MW01616791

Good With Money

A Brief Christian Guide to Financial Stewardship

John Carter

Foreword by Jonathan M. Wellum

2024

Front Cover:
"But so that we may not offend them, go to the lake and throw out your line. Take
the first fish you catch; open its mouth and you will find a four-drachma coin. Take it
and give it to them for my tax and yours." (Matthew 17:27).
All money is in God's account. Every last shekel at the bottom of the sea.

Back Cover:
"As he looked up, Jesus saw the rich putting their gifts into the temple treasury. He
also saw a poor widow put in two very small copper coins. 'I tell you the truth,' he
said, 'this poor widow has put in more than all the others. All these people gave their
gifts out of their wealth; but she out of her poverty put in all she had to live on.'"
(Luke 21:1–4).
Jesus exalted the generosity and faith of the widow. Her two mites represent the
importance of self-sacrifice to Jesus, who sacrificed far beyond His comfort for His
beloved sinners. Interestingly, the widow's giving of her two mites is the origin of the
expression "give my two cents."

ISBN   978-1-7382015-2-5

For Christians everywhere.
May we make the most of our time and money.
And may all glory be to God.

Acknowledgements

I am honored to now thank God for His providence, and for working through the spirit in everyone mentioned on this page to bring this book to fruition. I want to thank my wonderful wife Sheila for her nurturing companionship and all the advice she has offered me from the beginning. Among other things, she rightly suggested that I add some intrigue to the cover.

Pastor Alex Kloosterman has provided kind encouragement and fruitful conversation which have helped to shape parts of the book. He also pointed me in the direction of Jonathan Wellum, CEO of Rocklinc Investment Partners, who has gone out of his way to provide the foreword. Jonathan gave me encouragement and important feedback that led to a number of improvements. Pastor Ben Inglis also had a valuable influence through his friendship and editing.

The copy editing services of Meghan Visser, who is blessed with an eye for detail, have also been a great help.

Stephen North and Jacob Lemming offered the project a perfectly measured sip of commendation at a perfectly measured instance of time, by the grace of God. Thanks is also due to the uplifting friendship of Tim Clutton, a caring soul, and Ross MacLeod, a good old friend, and my best man. Darren and Brooke Roberts have also offered kind support.

Greg and Vashti Frankland, Rylan and Carleigh Auger, Jacob and Mikaela Leeming, Jack and Sunny Kehler, Jacob and Bernadette Taggett, Josh and Cheridan Perry, Matthew Madio, and Joseph McNabb have all greatly inspired me to raise financial hope for young adults.

Thanks also to my frugal friend Jerry Lane for our discussions about food finance, and for his lovingkindness. I am grateful for all of my brothers and sisters in Christ at Hill City Baptist Church for their outpouring of love and support.

I want to thank my father and mother for their loving sacrifices and support throughout my life. My sister Christine Carter offered much encouragement and useful feedback, after having enjoyed the book on a turbulent flight. Finally, I want to thank my son James Carter for giving me the inspiration to write this book. He likes to point out that he got the last word (see the last page).

Foreword

"Honor the LORD with your wealth, with the firstfruits of all your crops; then your barns will be filled to overflowing, and your vats will brim over with new wine" (Proverbs 3:9–10).

This admonition does not tell us to honor the Lord with our hymns of praise or with our prayers but with our wealth. Yes, we do honor the Lord when we lift up our voices in songs of praise and our hearts in supplication, but we can also honor the Lord with our wealth. For many Christians the idea of honoring the Lord with their wealth is not foremost in their thoughts, despite clear instructions found in God's Word. Christians are simply not aware of the significant number of Bible passages that speak on the topic of money and on managing their finances for the glory of God and for their eternal good.

In 1973, Howard Dayton, a successful businessman, began an in-depth study of the Bible and categorized all of the Scriptures that talk about money and possessions into a single topical index.[1] The result is a culmination of 2,350 Scripture passages that speak about money and our use of it. By way of contrast, there are 500 Bible verses that speak directly to the topics of faith and prayer. Why such a divergence? God knows that our attitude toward money is a barometer of our heart and our love towards God. Jesus told us that we cannot serve two masters. We cannot serve both God and money. Our Lord instructs us in Matthew 6:21: "For where your treasure is, there your heart will be also."

---

[1] Howard L. Dayton, Finances God's Way, compass1.org.

In Proverbs 3:9–10, Solomon is teaching his son that God must be at the center of his investment portfolio! Why? Because Solomon knew all too well that one of the major temptations in this life is to make money an idol and to love money more than our Lord! The apostle Paul in 1 Timothy 6:10 reminds us that "the love of money is a root of all kinds of evil." Money itself is neither good nor bad, but in our fallen world money can have and indeed does have a powerful influence on our hearts and can take us far away from the Lord. As Christians, it is critically important that the Lord has control over all our finances and that the principles we use to manage our wealth are consistent with the Holy Scriptures.

There are three basic truths I want to draw out from this passage. First, we are to honor the Lord with all our wealth. Honor in this context means to give gravitas or importance to the subject. This is a topic the son needs to take very seriously and it applies to all his wealth. Solomon is not speaking about a tithe! The emphasis is placed on *all our wealth* and the admonition is directly related to our relationship with the Lord. Why are we to honor the Lord with all our wealth? Because everything we have comes from Him. In Psalm 24:1 we read, "The earth is the LORD's, and everything in it, the world, and all who live in it." All we have comes to us from our sovereign Creator, the King of glory. The apostle Paul reminds us in 1 Corinthians 4:7: "For who makes you different from anyone else? What do you have that you did not receive? And if you did receive it, why do you boast as though you did not?" The only rational response for mankind is to honour the Lord with all our wealth!

Second, we are to Honor the Lord with the first fruits of all our increase. We have the responsibility and privilege to give to the Lord the first fruits. The first fruits take us back to Deuteronomy 26:1–10 and the deliverance of God's covenant people from slavery in Egypt. It is the faithful Lord who rescues His children from slavery and brings them into the promised land. Because of this they were commanded to give the first of their produce to God! Note they were not to give God their gleanings, or that which was left over, they were to give God His rightful due off the top! In this context, the first fruits was connected with the first exodus, the deliverance from Egypt. But for Christians today, how much more should we sacrificially give to God now that we have experienced His final and ultimate deliverance from sin through the substitutionary death of our Lord?

What do you do with what you are given?

Breathe, wealth,

Third, we are to live in faith that the Lord will provide for all our needs. In our passage we read, "then your barns will be filled with plenty and your vats will be bursting with wine." We are to give our best to God and trust that He will provide all we need. We are not to wait until our barns are full, rather we are to give in faith trusting God and His promises as we obey Him. God is trustworthy and His credit rating is better than triple A! The Scriptures attest to the truth that God is faithful to all His promises. In Matthew 6:33, Jesus tells His disciples to "seek first his kingdom and righteousness, and all these things will be given to you as well." Paul in Philippians 4:19 reminds us that "my God will meet all your needs according to His glorious riches in Christ Jesus." The context of this statement is very important. The Philippian church is showing great benevolence to Paul and being obedient to the Lord as they serve the Lord faithfully in the promotion of the gospel. In Malachi 3:8–10 the prophet warns the children of Israel not to rob God by not giving Him the full tithe. Rather, they are to bring the full tithe into the storehouse that there may be food in the house. God will not bless until we first give to Him in obedience and in faith.

When John Carter approached me about reading his new book on a Christian guide to finances, I was excited by the prospect. Sadly, there are only a few books written from a Christian perspective dealing with the day-to-day decisions that each of us must make when it comes to our finances. I was particularly intrigued by the fact that John was not a financial advisor but a scientist and mathematician by training and a business person professionally. Most importantly, he is a thoughtful Christian by practice. With this type of background, he is well positioned to cut through the usual financial jargon and speak directly to his audience in a language they can understand and, more importantly, put into practice.

The book is divided into six helpful sections. It begins by looking at giving, growing, and wasting your money. I loved the expression "A dollar saved is five dollars earned." You will have to read section one to find out what John means by this! The book continues with a very helpful section on taming your expenses. There is no question that one of the biggest challenges facing each of us in our consumer driven market is to control our spending and be more accountable to the Lord for our decisions. The third section deals with one of the most important investments a family can make and that is the real estate decision. John's expertise in this area comes through powerfully as he walks the reader through a helpful decision-making framework that should be considered when buying a home. Next there is a very helpful section on investing and the various asset classes that should be considered when building your own portfolio or looking to a professional to assist in the construction of your investment portfolio. The fifth section touches on the important topic of making it on your own and starting your own business. I was pleased that John tackled this important topic. Christians should be encouraged to be more entrepreneurial and to step out in faith by starting their own business. Christians need to be more forward looking regardless of the current horizon and trust in their heavenly Father who holds the future. Why are we not casting our bread upon the water when God promises that after many days we will find it again (Ecclesiastes 11:1)? The final section is a compilation of some helpful definitions of key financial concepts and some wonderful financial quotes and sayings that will both entertain and instruct.

Overall, John has written a wonderful guide on financial stewardship for Christians. He lucidly covers the range of essential topics in a manner that is easy to understand, follow, and implement. Throughout the book he interacts with biblical truths and principles, making sure the reader is always connecting the financial advice offered in the book with biblical principles. I highly recommend this book and personally found it very helpful. Even after almost 35 years in the investment industry, I was challenged and benefited greatly from the book.

Let me leave you with three final thoughts before you turn your attention to this helpful book:

1. You cannot take your money with you, but you can send it on ahead of you by faithfully serving the Lord and making sure it goes into God's ledger and into an inheritance that is imperishable, undefiled, and unfading, kept in heaven for you and guarded by God Himself. (1 Peter 1:4–5).

2. The time to honor the Lord with our wealth is today. Don't wait until you have more money but start immediately. It doesn't matter how much you have, you need to start right away. Honor the Lord with your wealth and the Lord will be faithful as He has promised.

3. Make the Kingdom of God and the propagation of the gospel of Jesus Christ your highest priority in your service and in your stewardship of your finances. Know where your money is going and focus it on ministries that are faithful to our Lord and His Word.

Jonathan M. Wellum
CEO of ROCKLINC
Investment Partners,
Elder at Trinity Baptist Church,
Burlington Ontario

Table of Contents

Preface

I once tagged along with a university friend to a student rooming house close to campus while he was searching for a place to stay for our senior year. I can remember the cool air of power emanating from the tall and trim landlord. Clothed in a perfectly tailored grey suit and clasping a sleek titanium briefcase, he carried himself with firm resolve into the kitchen where we had been waiting.

Having lived at home throughout university this was my first experience with the business of student housing. As I sat in a chair beside him, my friend signed the lease at the kitchen table. Having nothing else to do, I pondered the nature of the transaction taking place in front of me, and the whole student housing racket. I was thinking about the profit, the opportunity, and how I wanted to waltz around town like a big shot with a titanium briefcase in hand. Yes, I wanted to be a rich and powerful landlord someday. The warmth and beauty of that summer afternoon spent with a good friend in old downtown Toronto surely helped that idea take root.

My chance came in 2007. I had just earned my degree in biochemistry and math at the University of Toronto and was excited to be moving to Peterborough to attend teacher's college at Trent University along with my soon to be wife Sheila. We had saved up a down payment for a house and bought an old fixer-upper with good bones in a very opportune housing market. We rented three of the bedrooms, sharing the house with other students. This covered the mortgage with money to spare.

I soon found that teaching was not for me, but I took to the renovations of our old century house naturally and with zeal. I had found my calling. After six years, together with my wife, we had renovated four old houses and were providing rooms to house 19 students. We ran our student housing business for over nine years with near zero vacancy. It was a challenging and adventurous period in our lives. I thoroughly enjoyed working with my hands alongside my wife and getting to know the many students with whom we became friends over the years.

I was primarily driven by a sense of adventure, greed, and pride. In a city full of slums of student housing we carved ourselves out a niche by offering well-maintained, furnished, and decorated housing with cleaning services provided. We dealt primarily with older graduate students that appreciated the frequent presence of the landlord to help uphold an orderly shared living environment. I was proud to offer housing that I could honestly say I would be happy to live in myself.

Without Christ in my life, however, I couldn't manage my inflating ego, and the money that started flowing in got me too excited. I had been working constantly for years, but at the age of 32 my business was fully set up and producing a good cash flow. All needed renovations were complete, and I ran into trouble getting a mortgage for a fifth property to restore and then rent. The snowball I had been rolling and growing had hit a wall and I suddenly found myself without momentum, bearingless. I had little work to do to operate the business at that point. Effectively retired, that huge ego of mine, armed with idle hands, was not a good steward of the money I was getting through my God-given opportunity. That God-given opportunity was then revoked as I self-destructed in sin. Fortunately, I came out of the ordeal humbled rather than broke. I was led to Christ and am blessed to have received God's mercy. I retained almost all of what I earned in the business.

In large part, our housing business's success over the years followed from the proper management of finances. The same can be said of our personal finances since that time. Though my motivations were largely selfish then, it is my hope that the financial lessons I learned through business, as well as through my personal financial life over the years, can now be presented in a way that can give rather than take.

Help from God, a background in math and logic, and fortunate experiences in managing a business and family finances, have now led me to the authorship of this book.

For years I've cringed as I've watched friends make avoidable financial mistakes leading to the unnecessary loss of countless dollars, and altering the course of their lives. Now, as a Christian, I have been inspired to write this book to help people with their personal finances. Even if the reader were to gain just a few useful insights I would be joyful that God's good purpose has reached others, to His glory.

We are called to do good in the world (Ephesians 2:10). That good is the spreading of love through Jesus Christ, and in His name. We can accomplish this by making the most of our time. That means spending less of our time, and the money we make with it, carelessly, or on ourselves, and ensuring that our efforts don't go to unworthy causes. It is to this end that this book is ultimately written.

To begin with, we must acknowledge our need to labor if we are to produce wealth. Such fruitful productivity is a good thing. We are called to work if we are to sustain our own lives and be able to help out our brothers and sisters in need (2 Thessalonians 3:10–12). It is with this in mind that we will focus on stewarding the fruits of our effortful labor throughout this book.

Introduction

As Christians, we should approach the art of financial stewardship with committed effort and caution, knowing that we can not love both God *and* money (Matthew 6:24–26). However, wise money management need not be subject to the sin of greed. Though we should not labor for the love *of* money, we can labor to express our love *with* money. Using money as a means to selfishly serve lavish personal desires is unproductive. By such behavior, huge amounts of money continually becomes trapped in the black holes of insatiable egos. Looking at money as a means to serve the good purposes of God, however, is a good reason for employing the wisdom of effective money management.

We should look at money with a healthy degree of personal detachment, focusing with reverence on the good value it can bestow. Putting on the light yoke of Jesus Christ, we should aim to create an environment conducive to brotherly and sisterly love (Romans 12:9–21), rather than Lamborghinis parked in dark garages. By doing this we can reap the reward of joy rather than be plagued with an insatiable lust for *more*. That joy will surely shine brighter than any polish on a Lamborghini.

However, it should be mentioned here that the prevalent belief that *the rich are rich at the expense of the poor* is only sometimes the case (as in the rampant manufacture of inferior products for profit, and in the extreme case, the drug trade).[1] Many wealthy individuals have in fact benefited the world greatly by the contributions that have made them wealthy. Free capitalist markets that allow for the uninhibited production of value are a good thing, however, hoarding excessive wealth is not. If someone is blessed to bear the good fruit of God through a value producing innovation that has generated significant wealth for society and themselves, they are due no more glory than a hard-working plumber who has provided his life's hard work for a difficult and indispensable cause. All glory is God's, and so God calls us to take joy in His glory and be generous givers as we work for Him on the tasks given to us, whatever they may be.

If our acquired wisdom for money management blesses us with more than we need, we have a chance to make the world a better place. Here's a potentially fruitful scenario to consider: Perhaps you have noticed how hard some of your local roofers work to keep us well sheltered, often getting paid relatively little for a difficult and important job. Maybe you could arrange something with a local roofing company to ease the burden on the workers who have to pay for fall arrest training, tools, and work clothes. In your talks, the employers may themselves be moved to help their workers more. You could even help create a pay raise of a few dollars an hour, and of course include some nice Bibles with a note of thanks for their indispensable work.

We can be confident that money, being a placeholder for the value of work, has the potential to create change. The type of change that we create with it will either reflect the sin of greed or the goodness of love. It will determine whether that money will be wasted on vain pursuit or good fruit.

It is worth noting with emphasis that money can't buy happiness. This old adage is repeatedly confirmed by cases of unhappy millionaires. After our basic needs are covered, anything more just ends up being an empty promise. That is because (as Christians are blessed to know) true happiness can only come through love, and to the dismay of many, that is simply not for sale. However, money can certainly be a help to those who are not meeting their basic needs. That is where the goodness of God's charity can be delivered by those of us who have more than we need.

One question that I have heard asked a few times in my life speaks volumes. It goes like this, "Which would you prefer, many loving friends but not a single possession, or, everything in the world, as the only person in it?" I think most of us would choose the former. I have met many people with very little money who are loaded with the asset of highest worth: Love. These people seem quite content and, indeed, happier than many with large bank balances.

Remember also, no matter what way you cut it, there is ultimately only one true owner of anything, our Landlord: God. Whether we like it or not, we are all tenants here and all wealth is in His name, not ours. It can all be taken from us tomorrow by circumstances that are completely outside of our control. It is all in the hands of God, so let us be good stewards of His blessings.

A technical note is in order here regarding the examples that follow in this book. There is so much variability in what constitutes a "household," as well as between one household's circumstances and another's that any attempt at numerical precision would prove meaningless. Therefore, I have often rounded numbers for the sake of clarity while at the same time I have strived to give relevant, realistic, and informative examples based on the economy of America in 2023. U.S. dollars, and American Statistics are used throughout this book.

Part 1
Giving, Growing, and Wasting Money

Giving Money

Jesus said, "Again I tell you, it is easier for a camel to go through the eye of a needle than for a rich man to enter the kingdom of God" (Matthew 19:24). Though people will always try, it is hard to mince those words. God gave us His one and only Son, Jesus Christ. Should we refuse to give freely and with joy to His holy purposes? Should we hoard the spoils of our blessings for our selfish pleasures while others hunger for food or the Word of God? Unfortunately, this is something that can be very tempting to do.

Jesus beseeches us to deny ourselves, as He did (Matthew 16:24–26). He works for the salvation of others, rather than to secure comforts for Himself. In spite of this, many professing Christians argue against giving to the church of Christ and to those less fortunate than themselves.

Under the Law of the old covenant the "tithe" (the giving of 10% of one's income) was largely based on the funding of the tabernacle (later the temple), and the Levitical priesthood. Therefore, it is argued by some that because the early Christian church had no dedicated buildings (our bodies being the temple), and that because all Christians are called to be ministers of the gospel (1 Peter 1:13–20, 2:1–12), no funding should be required to uphold the new covenant.

While church buildings may not be *absolutely* required, they greatly help the church community congregate effectively and also provide a visible and publicly accessible entry point for non-Christians to be brought to Jesus Christ. Likewise, dedicated church pastors and administrators have an important role in a Christian's spiritual growth.

11

When Jesus sent out His seventy-two disciples as dedicated ministers of the gospel, He said to them, "... the worker deserves his wages ..." (Luke 10:7). Devoted ministers likewise need to be sustained.

Taken together, church buildings and clergy are two pillars that work to uphold the Christian faith and incur expenses that well warrant a tithe, if everything is to be financed properly. A tithe does, in fact, work out to be a reasonable sum to cover the financing of a typical church community.

Christian giving should not, however, be based exclusively on the calculation of an exact amount. Neither should it be bestowed to the church community as its only beneficiary. If someone is in need, we are called to help them if we can (Luke 3:11).

While the tithe is technically under the old covenant Law, and while Christians are not under the Law, the good of the Law should be *written on our hearts*. And while we are saved by grace alone and not by works, having been saved we naturally should strive to do those good works because we *want to*, not because we *have to*. As James says, "As the body without the spirit is dead, so faith without deeds is dead" (James 2:26).

It is also important to note that in His earthly ministry Jesus talks a lot more about helping the poor and needy than about the tithe given to the temple (Matthew 23:23; Luke 12:33). We therefore must look at how we can help the poor and needy *effectively*. You've probably heard it said, "Give a man a fish and he will eat for a day. Teach a man to fish and he will eat for a lifetime." There is no better way to help someone in need than by sharing the gospel. Not only will this help them establish their own livelihood, but will help others as they become a witness of the goodness of Jesus Christ.

While helping the poor and needy can at times be the mere giving of a meal, the giving of the Word can be the very cure to the disease of misery and poverty. To this end, the prayerful giving of Christian resources is a great way to help the poor and needy. This, coupled with provision and guidance in the use of earthly resources, can help to pull our struggling neighbors out of a life of despair into a life of fruitful productivity.

For various reasons, whether self-inflicted or circumstantial, countless people throughout history have fallen into a ditch. The solution is clearly not to keep throwing fish down to them through a socialist welfare system, but will be found in the loving help of Jesus Christ through a neighbor's extended hand.

It is disturbing how often professing Christians can be heard judging the poor and explaining why they should not be helped. Jesus came to save sinners. Jesus is the Just Judge, not us. We should follow His counsel rather than our own perceived wisdom. We shouldn't mince words to slither away from inconvenient truths, but follow Christ's very words, "Give to everyone who asks you, and if anyone takes what belongs to you, do not demand it back" (Luke 6:30).

It is surely a shame to say "no" to helping a downtrodden fellow sinner. Lamentably, we can find ourselves rationalizing our disobedience by twisting even the fundamental teachings of the gospel message to preserve our comforts.

Jesus repeatedly calls us to help those in need of either the Word of God, or of earthly resources. This should be indisputable because the call to help the needy resonates throughout the gospel message. God blessed us while we were still sinners (Romans 5:8). Are we not to try to act with the same mercy on our neighbors who are sinners like us? Our Lord, who wants us to follow His path of righteousness says, "But just as he who calls you is holy, so be holy in all you do; for it is written: 'Be holy, because I am holy'" (1 Peter 1:15–16).

The following Scripture passages are worth reviewing here:

The Sheep and the Goats, Matthew 25:31–46

"When the Son of Man comes in his glory, and all the angels with him, he will sit on his glorious throne in heavenly glory. All the nations will be gathered before him, and he will separate the people one from another as a shepherd separates the sheep from the goats. He will put the sheep on his right and the goats on his left.

Then the King will say to those on his right, 'Come, you who are blessed by my Father; take your inheritance, the kingdom prepared for you since the creation of the world. For I was hungry and you gave me something to eat, I was thirsty and you gave me something to drink, I was a stranger and you invited me in, I needed clothes and you clothed me, I was sick and you looked after me, I was in prison and you came to visit me.'

Then the righteous will answer him, 'Lord, when did we see you hungry and feed you, or thirsty and give you something to drink? When did we see you a stranger and invite you in, or needing clothes and clothe you? When did we see you sick or in prison and go to visit you?'

The King will reply, 'I tell you the truth, whatever you did for one of the least of these brothers of mine, you did for me.'

Then he will say to those on his left, 'Depart from me, you who are cursed, into the eternal fire prepared for the devil and his angels. For I was hungry and you gave me nothing to eat, I was thirsty and you gave me nothing to drink, I was a stranger and you did not invite me in, I needed clothes and you did not clothe me, I was sick and in prison and you did not look after me.'

They also will answer, 'Lord, when did we see you hungry or thirsty or a stranger or needing clothes or sick or in prison, and did not help you?'

He will reply, 'I tell you the truth, whatever you did not do
for one of the least of these, you did not do for me.'
Then they will go away to eternal punishment, but the
righteous to eternal life."

John the Baptist Making Straight the Way, Luke 3:11

"John answered, 'The man with two tunics should share
with him who has none, and the one who has food should do
the same.'"

It is safe to say that Jesus wants us to be generous givers as He is a generous giver. That means giving our time and money to the church and to those in need as best we can. Remember that when Zacchaeus pledged half of his wealth to the poor, Jesus was pleased (Luke 19:8–10). He did not look at it as a superfluous act. Jesus also commended the poor widow who in the temple gave two mites of her meager livelihood as an offering (Luke 21:1-4). We are not exhorted by Jesus to give nothing, or to stop giving at a defined amount. We are exhorted to give to our heart's content and, having been saved by grace, our heart's content will be found in giving.

A life of decadence simply cannot be reconciled with Jesus' many appeals to live selflessly and His exhortation to deny ourselves and follow Him past the point of comfort (Matthew 16:24–26). We might come up with every excuse under the sun to live a self-centered lifestyle, but the difficult truth will always remain. If we have an inanimate Ferrari in our garage that gives us more pleasure than helping someone in need by selling it, we are simply not following Christ's high calling. This admittedly can be a hard truth for our selfish hearts to embrace.

We need not fear or loath giving. God has, and will, provide for us in many ways (Matthew 6:25–34). With faith we must realize that our giving is not a dismal loss but a great opportunity to honor the Lord in obedience and thanksgiving and help our neighbors who are in need. We are promised that what we give will be rewarded in heaven's generous accounts, whereas all that we take for ourselves here on Earth will be left to die with the flesh, devoid of love (Luke 12:33).

"A generous man will himself be blessed, for he shares his food with the poor" (Proverbs 22:9).

Growing Money

You've probably heard it said that, "A dollar saved is a dollar earned." Yet for many people the truth is,

"A dollar saved is *five* dollars earned."

Read that statement again and think about it for a moment. Now let me explain the financial logic behind it.

If you have an average job, most of your earnings end up going towards basic living expenses that sustain you from one day to the next. There is a long list of these, a few of the big ones being: rent or mortgage-interest payments, grocery bills, car expenses, and utility bills.

These expenses, together with many others, will cost a typical family of four $85,000 this year (this figure does not include the mortgage principal component of mortgage payments, which is equity rather than expense, nor does it include any unnecessary expenses like entertainment).[2] By the end of the year that $85,000 will be gone with absolutely nothing left to show for it except survival. So, if your before-tax household income is between $105,000–$340,000, you will only be able to save between nothing and half of your pay (for high earners) after tax is paid.[3]

Consider a rather typical scenario. Suppose that total household expenses are $85,000, and after-tax household income is

$115,000 (which is what remains from about $150,000 of earnings after tax is paid). The rule of thumb, "A dollar saved is *five* dollars earned" applies here because for every five dollars of earnings, only one will be available to save.

For more insight into your household's unique circumstances, consider that, "A dollar saved is X dollars earned" where X is specific to you. To find out what X is for you, just work out this simple formula ("Yearly Expenses" should only include your basic living expenses, no discretionary expenses like restaurants, vacations, or the latest smart-phone):

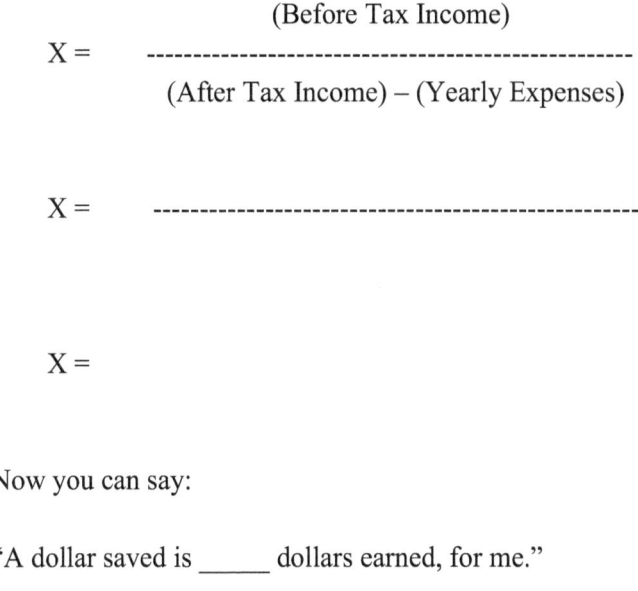

$$X = \frac{\text{(Before Tax Income)}}{\text{(After Tax Income)} - \text{(Yearly Expenses)}}$$

$$X = \text{---}$$

$$X =$$

Now you can say:

"A dollar saved is _____ dollars earned, for me."

For most of us, a dollar will only be available to save after anywhere from two to ten dollars have been earned. That is X = 2–10.

Hopefully you are starting to see that a saved dollar is no ordinary dollar.

A dollar saved is like the cream skimmed off the top of your earnings. Dollars such as these have been harmfully described as "disposable income," but it is far better to view them as "savable income." What is important here is that this understanding can help you look at your spending and saving habits more realistically. As we proceed, we will keep in mind that for a lot of families, "A dollar saved is representative of *five* dollars earned." It just can't be said enough.

Let's consider a simple example to drive the importance of this point home. Suppose you feel you'd like a new table saw in place of your old one after a sale caught your eye in the weekly hardware store flyer, "50% off!!! $250 for table saw!!!" Because this saw is something above your day-to-day necessary living expenses, you may have to earn $1,250 to properly cover the $250 to pay for the saw. Put another way, the saw will cost you the savings of $1,250 worth of labor. You can see how this often unused logic ("A dollar saved is *five* dollars earned") might change the way you think about money, and better inform the financial decisions you end up making as you begin to look at each dollar as having the potential to be a dollar saved.

Whatever your given station in life is regarding your vocation, there may be ways to bring in more dollars to your household. If you are working hard in a low paying job you should not simply view it as a failure of financial achievement, however. Many low-paying jobs are absolutely necessary. Surely the work of a roofer is no less righteous than that of a doctor. A high-paid doctor needs a roof over their head too. Low- and high-paid jobs need to be done in this world, so the answer to financial hardship cannot be the abandonment of low-paying jobs. If a low-paid job is your lot, take heart, your job is worthy.

That said, if you are wasting time binge watching Netflix, or playing video games, you should redirect your attention to your faith, family, and earning more money. You should strive to be productive.

Though you must understand its virtue, it is also important not to idolize work, and in so doing estrange your faith, friends, and family (which I have been guilty of doing in the past). Godly work is not measured by how many hours you can clock in a cubicle, but by the full array of your fruitful works of love, which should be directed towards work, home, community, and to God.

Ultimately, your financial life is a balancing act with your other God-given duties and blessings. There is no better way to learn to strike a good balance in it than by participating in your church community and reading your Bible. You can flip to Proverbs 10:4 and 14:23 right now to start.

You can grow money in three ways, by:

1. Earning more money
2. Losing less money (Parts 1–2)
3. Sowing seed: putting money to work by investing it (Parts 3–5)

Wasting Money

As John Bridges, Bishop of Oxford, said in 1587:

"A fool and his money are soon parted."

This has always been, and always will be, the case. A fool will spend his money carelessly, forgetting the work that was required to get it in the first place. He will not consider the optimal use of it, and instead dive headlong into emptying his wallet for the immediate gratification of his unbridled passions. He will live for selfish pleasures in the present moment. Time and again he will find that, after spending all of his money, he is no closer to happiness and likely much further away from it. A logical antidote to this folly is suggested by a Russian saying which observes that "spending is quick, earning is slow."

19

It is also of critical importance to realize that many financial fools have "expensive tastes." Expensive tastes can get you into a lot of trouble fast. Luxurious and fashionable possessions and decadent services offer only an empty promise of providing true happiness.

Many financial fools also try to, "keep up with the Joneses." This is always a losing battle. Fortunately, it is an unnecessary one. Don't try to live up to other people's often petty standards with money. Rather, try to live up to God's worthy standards for us through the responsible stewardship of money.

The best way to avoid being a financial fool is by acknowledging that "a dollar saved is *five* dollars earned" and thinking twice before spending hard earned dollars on the expensive tastes you may have. Seek joy in the Lord, and in the people in your life, places where it can be found. It will never be found by consuming *things*. **The ticket to happiness is love, given freely by Jesus Christ.**

Do you really need an ATV while you can't even pay your credit card balance as it is? If you have no savings and would like to buy a house someday (a worthy goal) why give up your lead by buying an unnecessary recreational vehicle? Even if you have a home and savings, you would still do well to ask yourself in all seriousness, "Can my money be put to a better use than an ATV?"

Essential bills and debts should all be covered before money is spent on unnecessary things. Even then, why spend money on unnecessary things? A Swedish proverb observes that, "If you buy what you don't need, you steal from yourself." Simply put, expensive tastes get in the way of saving up money that can be put towards worthy objectives, like home ownership or helping the needy.

Ensuring that our time and money don't go unnecessarily to those who don't really need them is a good way to follow our Lord. First and foremost, if we don't really need a product or service, we probably shouldn't pay for it. Whereas if we do need something, we should turn to those who are working hard as Christians to offer quality products or services.

You simply need to use some discretion and prayerful direction when choosing between product and service providers. We need to ask ourselves and the Lord some questions: Are we feeding large bank accounts, or stomachs? Are we giving to the greedy or to loving stewards of money? Are we buying things we don't even need?

22

Part 2
Taming Your Expenses

Home Improvements

Home renovation and remodeling can be cripplingly expensive. Can you rightly justify tearing out perfectly working and well-made kitchen cabinets only to replace them with possibly inferior but *new* ones at a cost of $10,000? *New* may only last you a few years. It might be much cheaper to wait until your old cabinets come back into vogue and just appreciate with gratefulness your well-made, well-working cabinets until then.

I was involved in renovating houses for over 15 years and yet I'll be the first to tell you, "if it ain't broke don't fix it" (or "upgrade" it). As with many things, there are exceptions to this, but renovations done to perfectly livable spaces where there is no functional benefit, and no intention of selling the house soon for a profit, are not worthy of the large expenses involved. There are a lot of costly things that you can do to your house that are unnecessary and that will not raise its value much. Don't assume that time and money spent on renovations are going to be reflected in property value (though this can be the case).

Beware of home remodeling TV shows, which can be dangerously seductive. They can easily lure you into such ideas as switching your kitchen backsplash from square to elongated tiles, or changing all of your light fixtures to the latest exposed-bulb fashion. You may start eyeing your faithful faucets with discontent, cringing over their now apparently ghastly chrome finish. Maybe you would feel better walking away from the hardware store with new ones in a brushed nickel finish, and a $1,000 receipt in your pocket. You would then surely feel a lot worse after watching the next episode of your favorite home remodeling show only to be informed that faucets in a matte black finish are now the way to go (who would have guessed that one?). So perhaps we would all be well advised to turn off those home remodeling shows, or watch them with a very critical eye.

On the other hand, home improvements that add to the utility of your home can be great investments. Adding a basement bachelor suite can bring in extra income from a tenant and add to the value of your house. Adding a second bathroom to a one-bathroom house is another example of added utility and value that will probably leave you ahead. Paying to keep your house in a good state of repair is also a worthy use of hard-earned money.

If renovations, remodelings, or repairs *are* in order, you may be able to "Do It Yourself" (DIY). DIY is a great idea when a task is within the scope of your abilities. If you have the aptitude for it, there is no reason why you can't complete tasks like installing a faucet, or hanging a new door. There are many resources (especially online) that you can use to learn how to do such things. The savings can be huge.

Consider the example of a faucet replacement. If you buy a faucet you like and then hire a plumber to install it, you can expect to pay about $300 just for the installation. Although the plumber may only get paid $75, between the service-call, the labor, the business expenses, and the company profit, the bill ends up being a number of times that amount. If you were to simply watch a few brief instructional videos online, follow the included instructions, and complete the task in two hours yourself, you will have effectively earned $150/hour. So maybe you should hire yourself as a DIY'er.

Don't assume that a professional will offer superior workmanship. Though this can be the case, oftentimes professionals can be apathetic, rushed, and sloppy. Of course, they want to get the job done without customer complaints, so their work will usually be sufficient, but few will go the extra mile. I've seen plenty of crooked toilets, poorly-run wiring, drafty windows, and sloppy drywall that has been professionally installed. You, however, will be careful and motivated to do a good job on your own property.

Whatever you do, be sure to stick to quality materials and workmanship. Trying to save money by using subpar building materials, or rushing the job by cutting corners, is self-defeating. If a job done right requires extra time and money, it's worth every minute and dollar. Do it right the first time.

One thing is for sure, if you want to stay "fashionable" by remodeling your home, you may find yourself "fashionably-late" owning it.

Car Ownership

The car is an amazing machine that the average person has only had access to over the last ninety years. Now, in our modern world, driving a car is almost unavoidable. As you know, a lot of bills come with driving a car: gas, insurance, maintenance, and depreciation (which is the yearly reduction in the value of your car as it makes its way to the auto-wreckers). Taken together, keeping a car on the road costs on average about $12,000 a year as of 2023.[4]

Since car ownership is considered a common day-to-day *necessary* expense, the rule "a dollar saved is *five* dollars earned" does not apply here (the money of the expense has no potential for savings). You will, however, probably have to earn about $16,000 to foot all of the bills for the car as well as cover the corresponding income tax. The take-home message here is that driving a car is *very* expensive. I've heard it said that, "cars keep the poor poor," and there is truth to that.

Let's now look at what can be done to steward your car finances wisely to reduce your expenses. First and foremost, you should be aware that a brand-new car loses about 10% of its value the moment you drive it off the dealership lot. So, you would save 10% of the car's new retail price by simply buying a year-old car (all told, you would pay roughly 20% less than the price at the dealership for a one-year-old car once the one year of depreciation is also factored in). For an average car, that 10% savings amounts to almost $5,000.[5] Needless to say, you might want to consider buying a used car.

Buying a used car is not just a good idea because of the immediate savings, however. Insurance is cheaper on a used car. Also, although you will find reviews and opinions of new car makes and models, the truth is that no one really knows how a new model will perform until a few years have passed. So, when you buy a new car you really have no idea if it will be a good value or a lemon. Consider buying a make and model that has been on the road for a few years and has proven its worth. I can tell you that the 2007 Toyota Corolla is known to run a very long time with minimal maintenance.[6] Ours is well on its way to 400,000 km, and that is music to my ears.

You may think that by buying a new car you will be avoiding many problems. Perhaps you've had some hassles with used cars you've owned in the past (or present) and are looking forward to owning a new car. Well, I can assure you that the moment you buy a new car it will become a used car.

I have a story to tell you. We have a friend who bought a new car that failed after just a few years. Then they bought another new car that failed after a few more years. Over the course of a decade, they lost about $50,000 (the cost above driving a reliable used car model in that time). They have been unable to get into the housing market to this day, but have started buying reliable used car models instead of expensive new car models of unknown reliability. Needless to say, a $50,000 loss early in life can greatly stunt your progress.

If you have the money, buy your car without a loan. Or, if you have a loan on it, get out of it if you can. Dealers may try to convince you that a car loan is a good deal. However, it is just more debt. Even if the debt is at a low interest rate, why bother encumbering yourself with more debt liability if you don't have to?

Lastly, why pay a ton of extra money for a "cool car" just because you like how it looks? If you pay $15,000 more than is actually needed for a car because of an untreated case of "expensive taste," that money is going to come out of your potential savings. Yep, you may only get $1 saved for $5 earned. That is, you'll be working away to earn $75,000 to produce enough "cream" (savings) to cover the cost of the "cool look." Maybe you should buy a cool $10 bumper sticker instead, if it will save you from this costly folly.

Food

We all need to eat, and an average American family of four spent at least $12,000 on food in 2023.[7] This makes food one of the top three life expenses (together with housing and transportation).

With many of life's necessary expenses there is rather little wiggle room for savings. This is not the case with food however. Food expenses can vary greatly depending on how you purchase it. Although the average family will spend $12,000 on food this year, that cost can vary between half to double that amount. That is, between $6,000 to $24,000 (and there is no upper limit if you like dining out). Where you fall in that range hinges on the decisions you make.

If you want to get closer to the lower end of that range, while your family is still eating a healthy diet, there are a number of ways you can achieve this:

1.   Don't scrape food into the garbage. The average family of four threw away over $1,500 worth of potentially edible food in 2023.[8] A lot of food waste is from fresh produce like fruits and vegetables after they spoil (so plan your meals carefully). Another major factor contributing to food waste is tossing edible leftovers instead of committing to eating them later on.

Perhaps your children are picky eaters. Give them a worthy life lesson by not giving in to what they want. Remind them to be grateful with what they have been given rather than pampering to their preferences. They can eat it now or wait until they are actually hungry. They won't starve just because they didn't get their first choice. They may put up a stand at first to gain control, but if you don't surrender to them they won't press the matter, and will come out the better for it.

In today's world many parents are letting their children call the shots. This is producing attitudes of entitlement as well as developing unrealistic expectations that the world around them will always yield to their desires. It also fosters selfishness as the child comes to see that everything revolves around their wants rather than the needs of others. This all amounts to a great disservice to children. Although taking a stand may be uncomfortable as a parent, if we love our children, we must show it by difficult means at times, remembering that very often the best thing for a child is not what they want.

2.   Restaurant dining and fast-food are probably even more expensive than you think. If you eat out as a family at a typical restaurant for just one meal a week and also get drive-through fast-food just once a week, this can easily add up to over $8,000 a year. That's $6,000 more than had you prepared meals at home. Because dining out is unnecessary, $30,000 in income earnings may be required to generate the savings needed to properly cover those biweekly meals out on the town.

It is a good financial exercise to sit down and tally up the small amounts we hand over at drive-throughs over a week and then multiply accordingly to account for a full year's expenditure to see how much we are actually spending on fast-food (try it).

Suppose you get a fast-food lunch for a mere $15 each weekday, big deal right? That works out to about $4,000 a year for clogged arteries, and may cost all of the savings you can muster from $15,000 of your earnings (it will be about $3,000 more than food prepared at home). Something cheaper, healthier, and more meaningful can surely be found to give you the fulfillment you seek. A picnic at the park, a BBQ in the yard, or tea on the porch can be every bit as enjoyable, or more so, than a restaurant or fast-food meal. So consider saving the money and your health.

3.   It is a blessed thing in life that many of the most expensive foods are also unhealthy for you, and therefore not needed. So clear your plate of them and save money as you become healthier. It's a win-win situation. Expensive and unhealthy foods include snack foods, processed foods, and alcoholic beverages. This is not to say you must cut these things out entirely, but there may be plenty of room to cut back on these while reaping only benefits. When you eat unhealthy foods often, not only do you lose money and clog your arteries, but you also derive less satisfaction from them because they become a norm. The following list of cheap and expensive grocery items may help you to better economize your food expenses (there is a cut-out copy on page 119 at the back of this book):

Economy of Grocery Items

Cheap Healthy Foods	eggs
potatoes/sweet potatoes	chicken (whole, legs, drumsticks)
peas	cottage cheese
dried pasta	yogurt
broccoli	peanut butter
carrots	**Expensive Foods**
canned tomatoes	fresh meats (especially red meats)
frozen mixed vegetables (bulk pack)	cheeses
rice	snack foods
oatmeal	prepared foods (i.e., potato salad)
bread	frozen breaded chicken or fish
canned beans (dried or canned)	fruit (out of season)
bananas	cut fresh fruit
frozen berries (bulk pack)	alcoholic beverages

4.   My friend Jerry recently said, "If I'm having cucumber every day and it's been $1/pound, and it's $6/pound this week, I'm not having cucumber this week. You've got to plan your meals around sales." He makes a good point there. It is certainly true that careful planning of food purchases utilizing sales and coupons can save you money. If you've got the time and you haven't got much wiggle room financially, the effort will be well worth it *if* you are aware of several common

consumer pitfalls that can end up costing rather than saving you money.

Us humans often simply cannot resist what we see as a "good deal." We end up buying things that we don't even need at all because they are 50% off. Well 50% off is 100% too much money for an unneeded item. We must realize that there are no "good deals," only "bad deals" on things we don't need. Food ends up getting thrown out or added to bellies as unnecessary calories because of excited lapses in judgement summoned by "good deals." You may say, "well, that's not me, I'm not stupid," but we can all get deceived in this way. I know that I'm prone to it.

Wild scallops might be 60% off this week. But before you celebrate your shrewd cunning in pouncing on the deal, consider that if the sale price is $12/pound, that that is still exorbitantly expensive compared to alternatives and an unnecessary addition to your freezer.

You must spend time on flyers and coupons if you want to eke out significant savings. As you've heard it said, "time is money." Even more than this, "time is your life." We want to save money, but we don't want to waste time to save a few dollars here and there if our spare time may already be very limited. Reserving sufficient time for family, reading Scripture, and prayer is an important consideration when deciding when to divert our efforts to saving.

Flyers can also end up sending us on extra grocery store trips if we're not careful. Not every store will price-match and it doesn't make sense driving across town to save $5 if 30 minutes and $10 in mileage on our car are required. Yet we can end up being lured into this sort of thing when we get our nose in a flyer.

It must be emphasized here that there are certainly many people who can manage flyers and coupons masterfully, using apps like "Flipp" to reap financial benefit, but be aware that the judicious use of flyers and coupons is not always straightforward. You want to avoid unnecessary purchases, save time for worthy things, and minimize costly grocery store trips. You will do well by planning your meals carefully and purchasing only the food that you need with laser-focus in the store. Flyers and coupons can be used beneficially in doing this *if* you are careful.

There are two "deals" that I feel compelled to point out here. Costco's time-honored deal on a rotisserie chicken, and the hotdog and drink at the Costco food kiosk, are exceptional bargains. No, I am not affiliated with Costco, I just can't withhold disclosure of these particularly great "loss-leader" deals from whoever does not know about them.

5. It makes sense to quickly cross check unit prices on similar items. The unit price can be found on many product labels below the item price. You may be able to quickly save some money, but be careful that you do not submit to buying a product you don't like or that is priced lower for a good reason. Remember the old adage, "You get what you pay for," which is often the truth.

6. Check expiry dates. Grocery stores try to keep items closest to expiry at the front. So if you don't want to drink four liters of milk in two days, be aware of the expiry date. My grocery savvy friend Jerry will bring almost expired items to the checkout and ask for a discount on them. Apparently, he often gets large discounts. This makes sense because the store is about to take a loss on them and the manager or owner has the authority to lower the price, so the discount is a great synergy between the store and the shopper.

7. Buying food and other staples at bulk stores can be a good idea. You will save money on things that you use a lot of. You will also lose money on things that you don't use a lot of, so be careful. Nonperishable items like toilet paper and paper towels are a perfect fit for bulk buying. A bulk box of four

cartons of orange juice will save you money if you have room in the fridge and you go through a lot of orange juice. Maybe a bulk bag of frozen vegetables would also be a good idea.

8. It may be worthwhile to keep a chest freezer, like my frugal friend Jerry does. There are a number of pros and cons involved with chest freezers that need to be considered, however. Savings realized by keeping a chest freezer depend on your particular family size, eating habits, self-discipline, and aptitude for organization.

The main pro is that you can utilize bulk buying prices. Here are the cons, however: The upfront cost to purchase the freezer, the space used in your home for the freezer, the potential losses during power outages or freezer failures, the electricity cost to run the freezer (about $50/year), which is a surprisingly small but still notable expense), and the tendency to misjudge your needs when buying large quantities of food. This last error can be a big problem. I know that a lot of chest freezer food intended to save money never gets eaten and is thrown out freezer-burned after a few years.

Making a few bad choices on bulk purchases can render a chest freezer a liability rather than an asset. Some people will no doubt save over $1,000/year using them while others will lose over $1,000/year using them.

Utility Bills

Heat, hydro, and water bills are significant household expenses. Taken together, the average American household spent about $4,200 on these services in 2023.[9] This number includes many single or two person households in small apartments or condos, however, and will be higher for an average family of four living in a detached house.

Let's assume that your utility bills also add up to $4,500. Unfortunately, you would be hard pressed to reduce this number by more than 25% through even the wittiest and most severe conservation efforts. This is because most of your utility consumption is inseparable from your normal routines. So, while you may manage to scrape together savings of $1,000 by a year of much annoyance, ask yourself, will it be worth living with cold showers and a house that is two degrees less than comfortable? Would you perhaps lose over $1,000 of productivity as a result of the time-consuming hassle of the savings?

There are, however, a few ways to save some money on utilities without the punishment of undue troubles. Using low-flow shower heads, replacing old toilets (pre-1992)[10], and installing sufficient attic insulation and proper door weather-stripping will probably end up saving you more than you spend in the effort.

A sizable portion of your hydro bill comes from hot water. If you have an electric hot water tank, you can install a timer so that you can heat your water during the cheap "off-peak" hours. A hot water tank timer can save a family of four over $150 a year, and it all happens automatically. These devices cost about $50 and can provide automatic savings year after year (though you will have to remember to reset them during daylight saving time and power outages along with all of your other clocks). Over a 20-year period you could save over $3,000 after spending a few hours to purchase and install the $50 unit. Make sure also that your hot water tank is well insulated. You can buy an insulating jacket for it for under $50 at the hardware store.

Keep in mind that you may never break-even on some of the more expensive upgrades to the energy efficiency of a house. Or, it may take decades for them to merely pay themselves off. For example, if your old windows are well sealed and weather-stripped, it may take the rest of your life and then some to pay off the cost of new ones with the marginal annual energy savings they provide (which was approximately $100/year for the average sized houses we upgraded between 2007 and 2016). Though new windows will increase the value of your house, if you are not selling it, be aware that you will be transferring funds into something that will give you little payback until you sell (and by then, they may be "old" once more, leaving you at a loss).

Currently, in America, the break-even point for the cost of solar panels is about nine years.[11] That is how long it will take to simply *break even*. That is a long time waiting on a lot of money that could have been earning profit invested elsewhere. Though many models claim to have a 25-year life expectancy there is no assurance of this, and recouping your expense would be dubious if you were to sell your house before the break-even point.

Another way to save money is to avoid pitfalls with your appliances. Many people throw aside their old, energy-inefficient, yet *working,* appliances for costly new, energy-efficient ones. There are a number of factors which often get overlooked in the financial (as well as environmental) logic here. Foremost is that it will actually take many years for the savings in energy expenses to add up to the price of the new appliance. On top of this, many new appliances (despite advertised claims to the contrary) aren't lasting for those many years needed to reach that break-even point.

I have seen friends go through a number of refrigerators at the cost of many thousands of dollars while I've had my older model all along. They have saved hundreds of dollars on electricity and lost thousands of dollars on fridges.

A typical 20-year-old fridge from the early 2000's is likely to use around 530 kWh per year and will cost about $80 per year in electricity to run (at $0.15/kWh). A newer, more energy-efficient fridge, however, might only use 350 kWh annually (almost 40% less energy) and cost about $50 per year to operate. So, by upgrading your fridge you'll save about $30 each year.[12] That small yearly savings is not going to cover the loss you'll incur by getting rid of your old working fridge, which has been paid for, and paying a large sum for a new fridge.

Even environmental motivations to switch to new energy-efficient appliances can be unfounded. This is because the energy required to source the materials, manufacture, and ship the new appliance, as well as remove the old working appliance, is significant. This energy is called the "embodied-energy." A typical refrigerator has about 1,600 kWh of embodied-energy.[13] So, in the example of the replacement of a 20-year-old fridge given above, if your new fridge were to last less than 8 years, the savings in energy realized by its efficient operation will be eclipsed by the energy expended to produce and ship it. In other words, not only may a new energy-efficient fridge cost you more money than it saves, but there is also a good chance that it may end up using more energy than it saves. The claim of "energy saving" can in fact end up being "pocket draining."

When your old appliance has failed, however, a new energy-efficient model can then sensibly take its place.

As we consider our use of utilities, it is important to note that were the costs of energy and water resources to increase significantly (a frightening but very real possibility), there would be a corresponding increase in compensation for conservation efforts.

Thrift Clothing

In my experience there is no better way to put together your wardrobe than shopping at thrift stores. You will often find brand new clothing at a third of the cost of retail, or less. Some of the best clothes I've ever owned have come from thrift stores. The selection at some of these stores can also be extensive because most garments in stock are not alike. Therefore, in a single shopping trip you may be able to fulfill a lot of your clothing needs.

I believe that thrift store clothes shopping is altogether better than running around to pricey and limited brand name clothing stores. Consider buying brand name clothing after it has simply been taken from the retail hanger to the thrift store hanger.

Charitable thrift stores are also a great destination for your unneeded clothing. Don't throw it out.

Sales

As with grocery flyers and coupons, "sales" on other goods and services can easily bring about a financial loss rather than a gain if you're not careful. We can be tricked into immediately thinking, "good deal!" when we see, "sale!". Though a sale can very well offer a good deal to you, it can very well be a bad deal in hiding. Remember that Swedish proverb, "If you buy what you don't need, you steal from yourself."

I'll repeat here that if something is on sale at 50% off, it is 100% too much money if you don't need it. Sales tend to bend our rational thinking and can lead to unneeded purchases and other costly behaviors. I'm reminded of seeing cars lined up down the road at gas stations with drivers waiting to save a few dollars. Just imagine the time these deal seekers forfeit and the depreciation they incur on their idling cars. Maybe they will come out of that gas station a few dollars ahead, but they'll never get that half hour back.

When confronted with an enticing sale, a good idea would be to ask yourself the questions, "Do I really need this?", and, "Haven't I been living well enough without it?" Another good idea would be to sleep on it before making a decision. If time is on your side, use it. If the sale is on for a week, don't let the fear of an empty shelf drive you to rash measures. You don't have to think about it too much, the matter will turn itself over in the back of your mind. After a few days you may be surprised to find that you have absolutely no interest in the sale item. When it comes to any costly decisions in life, it is always a good idea to deliberate if time permits. This sensible approach is akin to letting the smoke clear before taking aim at a target.

Quality Goods and Services

I remember hearing one man say, "I can't afford it, it's too cheap!" while talking about the "too good to be true" price on an appliance. I thought that was a good way to express the worthy cost of a quality product. To save a few dollars many people are lured into choosing products that quickly fail. It costs a lot more to buy three $50 pairs of shoes than one $90 pair of shoes (and think of the hassle incurred by having to continually replace bad products). It may not always be true, but chances are, "you get what you pay for."

I use online reviews, reputation, and advice from friends to get a good sense of the quality of a product. The most important thing is to verify by various means that a product is a good one before you buy it. I know I've bought a few things in the past thinking I was getting a good deal only to find myself dropping a bad deal straight into the garbage.

Quality Goods Used

While garage sales and thrift stores may turn out to be good places to find deals, there are a few drawbacks to using these venues. The biggest problem is that you are shopping around blind, not knowing what the stock of a garage sale or thrift store will hold (an exception is thrift store clothing which, as previously mentioned, is usually well stocked, making thrift stores a reliable destination to find clothing you can use at a great price). This can waste a lot of time. Also, we can be inclined to make unnecessary purchases at garage sales and thrift stores, as interesting as they are to search through.

Online thrift marketplaces, however, like Facebook Marketplace, and Ebay Classifieds are easily searchable with huge stock available, so you can effectively track down what you need at a fraction of the retail price, and in a fraction of the time. You will also avoid getting sidetracked by things you are not actually looking for.

Why buy a new couch for instance when you can get a nice quality made one for half the price because someone is "remodeling" their home a year after buying it? You can save thousands on furniture, appliances, and tools in just a few minutes by sleuthing around the online used marketplaces when needed.

Penny Pinching

Many people who lived through the era of the great depression became more grateful for the things that they had. Out of necessity they were very careful with every penny. These people learned to be "frugal," or "prudent," with their money. At that time frugality and prudence were rightly considered virtues. Now, however, "frugal" and "prudent" have become synonymous with terms like "penny pincher" and "miserly," which carry connotations of terrible vice. I would propose that "penny pinching" has both its virtues and its vices.

Gratitude is a virtue that does not come naturally to many of us. We tend to take things for granted, lacking thanksgiving for our blessings, when we have plenty of money to play with. Whereas we tend to become more thankful for what we have when living with increased limitations.

If we have plenty of money to toss around, limits can be put in place with intentional effort on our part, rather than out of the necessity brought upon us by poverty. Otherwise we are apt to develop the ungrateful disposition that can accompany a lifestyle of decadence. That's not to say that we should live in a self-imposed state of extreme poverty, but we can not only benefit ourselves, but also those in need, with the resulting saved funds derived from a life of contented sufficiency.

Living a life where we get whatever we want, whenever we want is a recipe for ungratefulness and all manner of spiritual harm. We can give our praise to God with a genuine spirit, however, if we are truly aware of the value of the things that we are blessed to have.

On the other hand, spending large amounts of time worrying about small savings can also be a vice. It will certainly not get you very far financially.

A good compromise here might be to be a "dollar pincher" rather than a "penny pincher." Make the most of money, but not by wasting your time worrying away trying to save a penny here and a penny there, but by "ball parking" prices a little bit while still keeping things under a watchful and caring eye.

Wise by the Penny, a Fool by the Pound

You certainly don't want to be "Wise by the penny, a fool by the pound." This old saying describes those who instead of focusing on the big picture, zero-in on the pennies. It is the financial equivalent of the old adage that warns, "Don't miss the forest for the trees." Even if you can get those pennies clear in your focus, you'd be better off zooming out to look at the things that will have larger consequences for your finances.

I am reminded here of a friend from university who would fret over things like the cost of trendy clothing. He would do things like shop through many stores trying to save a dollar or two. All the while I couldn't help thinking, "You don't even need those clothes, so they have no value at all." So while he would squeeze out a few dollars in savings, he lost a lot of his money on an expensive habit. He was being "penny wise, but pound foolish."

Another example of this folly happens all the time when people indiscriminately hire the company that gives them the cheapest possible quote to do work on their house. They may save $1,500 on a

$10,000 job, but then have to pay for the $10,000 job all over again in a year. If roof shingles that will last twice as long are going to cost only 20% more, go with them. Likewise, if a reputable company with a good track record of quality workmanship is going to cost you 20% more, consider going with them. Do it right the first time.

Budgeting

Budgets can help you to see more clearly where money is going and therefore reduce the uncertainties which may be causing you undue stress. By simply preparing a budget you will learn a lot about how much money you are spending on different products and services.

The idea behind a budget is that once you have set it up by dividing your funds into various categories, you will be able to follow defined limitations and track your expenses, leading to a more financially organized life.

However, because budgeting can be time consuming and a bit of a hassle, many people simply won't do it. Though I would recommend at least attempting to make a basic budget, and then progressing to a more detailed one (if only to acquaint yourself more fully with your financial activity), the truth is that a budget, while very helpful, is not absolutely imperative to financial success. In fact, an even better way to manage money is to simply not buy anything you don't really need.

No budget can actually help you to manage your necessary expenses because, if they are necessary, you simply cannot avoid them one way or another. With what remains after those necessary expenses are paid, if you simply follow sound principles of financial wisdom in all of your spending and saving, you will do equally well with or without a detailed budget. That said, sound principles of financial wisdom are easy to lose sight of without a budget.

If you are struggling just to stay afloat financially, a budget is more important because it can help keep you out of debt. In this case, by putting things into a clear perspective, a budget will help you to make tough decisions about what is truly necessary. A commonly perceived necessity like internet service might have to be axed in unfortunate circumstances, and the use of a library computer substituted for it. You may have to jog to your gym and back instead of paying for a membership there. And you may have to switch to more affordable service providers.

If you decide to forgo the informative practice of budgeting, at the very least try looking over a few months of your credit card statements, bank statements, and grocery receipts (which are itemized). Look at what you've bought and how much it cost. Think carefully about where money is going and identify any expensive habits that you can do without.

If you are interested in drawing up a budget, consider this simple template and try making up a similar one to start (you can also use the template on page 117 at the back of this book, which can be cut out):

Basic Budget

Expense	Monthly Cost
Mortgage/Rent	
Groceries	
Car Gas	
Property Tax	
Utilities	
Home Maintenance	
Home Insurance	
Car Insurance	
Car Maintenance/Depreciation	
Tithe	
Clothing	
Phone	
Internet	
Professional Fees	
Gifts	
Other	
Savings	
Monthly Total	
Annual Total	

Managing Debt

An old Yiddish saying reminds the lender that "interest grows without rain." This, however, is not good news for the borrower (debtor), as it will be their blood, sweat, and tears that will sustain the money lender's crop. A good saying to consider for those tempted to borrow would be, "Avoid debt like the plague."

Oftentimes, especially when you are a student or starting out with a young family, debt of various forms will be essential. A student loan, a mortgage, or a business loan may be needed. If managed well, debt can be the means to considerable financial success in life. Most successful businesses have utilized debt as a means to start and grow. However, you don't want to take on debt if you are not going to seriously commit to the money you borrow by putting it to good use under your watchful eyes, and skilled, hardworking hands.

The worst kind of debt is consumer debt generated by expensive tastes. As we've discussed, expensive tastes would be best nipped at the taste bud. Going into debt because you really want the latest smartphone to waste more time on social media, for instance, is simply not a good idea.

Avoid credit card debt in particular. Though credit cards are useful, unless you find yourself in a financial emergency, your aim should be to pay off the entirety of the balance with each monthly bill. Credit card interest rates can be menacingly high, often over 20%. If you're only making minimum payments, interest will start being charged on top of interest every month. You will end up growing an out-of-control compounding snowball of debt.

If you have student loan debt, pay it off quickly. If you are currently a college or university student, borrow as little as possible, steering clear of sin. Don't be like the prodigal son who squandered all his money (Luke 15:11–32). Be *careful*, and consider getting a part-time job, if only for a few hours a week (if that's all you can manage alongside your studies). Any money that you can scrape together will help.

How much money you earn, and how much debt you take on from age 16–26 will have a huge effect that will echo into your future. More than any other time, that decade will set the stage for the rest of your life. If you are young and reading this let me assure you that you will do very well by focusing serious effort towards your education and earnings. Often, those that float around in their early years doing whatever they want in the process of "finding themselves" end up completely "losing themselves." This is a common example of the deceitfulness of sin, which is usually a complete inversion of the truth.

Part 3
Real Estate

Real Estate

The best investments that I have ever made have been in residential real estate (housing), and in this I am not alone. One of the things that I like most about owning real estate is that it gives you *real estate*, not just a promise on a note of paper. You can live in a house, and everyone needs to live somewhere. This arguably makes a house the best asset you can own, and therefore a worthy place to invest money (if the price is right).

Buying a house gives you a home of your own, but it can also benefit you in many other ways:

1. By making monthly mortgage payments (if you need to borrow from a bank, as most young homeowners do) instead of monthly rent payments (that completely disappear), you will be building up equity in your house. After a while you will have paid off the mortgage altogether. In this way, buying a house with the help of a mortgage can set you up on a routine of forced monthly savings. Left to our own devices, most of us will not have the self-discipline or know-how to build up savings without such forced payments.

2. If times get tough, or you would like to pocket some extra money, a house always gives you the option of renting out a room to a boarder (like a university student). Or, if you buy a house with a separate basement suite (which is a great idea) you can get your house to carry some of its own weight by renting to a tenant. Though this may not be something that

sounds too appealing, the option is valuable. If things go south for you, or if family or friends need help, you may be very glad to have a house with a basement suite.

3.   Later in life, if you haven't managed to save much for retirement but own your house, you can always borrow money from it. One way of doing this is through a "reverse mortgage." As the term implies, a reverse mortgage is the opposite of a mortgage. Instead of buying a house by borrowing a large sum and making monthly payments, you receive monthly payments which over time bring you back to the beginning with a large sum owed, which can be paid off by the sale of the house. This way, you can get the needed equity out of your house while also living in it until most of that equity is exhausted.

4.   A house also gives your life a higher degree of security and freedom. You will not have to worry about a landlord evicting you because he is getting ready to sell the house and wants to renovate it, for instance. Also, you have little freedom to make changes to a property you don't own.

Buying Your First House

To buy your first house you will need a good chunk of saved money. A plan for getting this is laid out on page 81 (to best understand it you will need to learn a few things first though).

If you are planning on buying a house, it would be informative to start looking through your local real estate ads and real estate websites, through which you can access listings of houses for sale in your area together with detailed information about each listing. This will familiarize you with local market prices as well as home features you should be considering.

What a House Should Cost

You can't change the market prices of the housing in your area, but you might find it revealing to assess the value of housing from a different perspective than market price alone. Below are four common methods of calculation by which the value of a house can be gauged:

1. **Market Value:** The price people are buying houses for. In one sense, a house is only worth what someone is willing to pay for it.
2. **Investment Value:** The value of the house as a reflection of how much rental income it can generate as an investment. A house price of about ten times its annual gross rent is usually reasonable from an investor's standpoint.
3. **Building and Land Cost:** The cost to actually build a house. This includes all material costs, labor costs, and land and planning costs.
4. **Income Ratio:** Over the last 75 years, houses have cost on average roughly five times median annual household income in the US and the UK.[14] This has also been the case in Canada over the last 25 years.[15] Given that this trend has proven consistent and economically viable over many years, it is reasonable to expect a house to cost about five times median household income.

Now you can use each evaluation method to get an estimate of current home values (rather than looking at current home prices alone).

For those who are not homeowners and are currently discouraged by home prices, I want to offer some words of hope. House prices can undergo declines. Sometimes during a housing market correction, prices can swing below even rational levels (as in the 2007 subprime mortgage crisis). So be careful to save up, not wasting money on unworthy *things*, but also not neglecting God His worthy due. You want to be posed to take advantage of home purchase opportunities when they come knocking. You will certainly never be able to buy a house if you don't start saving for one.

Mortgages and Down Payments

The first step to home ownership is to figure out how you are going to pay for a house. It is usually the case that you will have to borrow money from a bank to pay the full price of a house. Such a loan is called a mortgage. To get a mortgage, you will have to pay at least 3% of the house price with your own money.[16] This is called a down payment.

Banks are in the business of lending money so that they can make money, and they make that money by charging you interest on the loan you receive from them. The size of the loan, the interest rate on the loan, and the timeframe over which you agree to pay it back are all terms that will have to be agreed upon to make a mortgage contract with a bank.

Before you even begin to look for a house, you will want to figure out how much money you can scrape together to buy one. That is where a mortgage broker comes in.

Using a Mortgage Broker

One of the best ways to get started on your house purchase is to consult a reputable independent mortgage broker. They will charge a fee, but this will probably be well worth it if they are a skilled mortgage broker. Though many people go straight to their own bank to inquire about a mortgage, thinking that they will get the best deal there, this almost never turns out to be the case.

Banks do not reward loyalty as one would intuitively think, so why reward them with your business when you can look around for the best deal? The mortgage market is so large that the chance that your personal bank will get you the best deal at any given time is very slim. This is where a mortgage broker comes in. Their job is to serve you, not the banks. So ideally, they will be on your side, finding you a lender and helping you work out the best terms for your mortgage contract.

A mortgage broker may also be able to get a mortgage set up for people who would not qualify for a mortgage at any of the big banks. There are lending companies as well as private lenders who will provide mortgages to those with less-than-ideal credit histories or income. They usually charge a higher interest rate to cover the increased risk that they are taking, but this may be a good compromise to consider for some people. If you are looking for such an unconventional mortgage, be sure to take on the responsibility of working hard to honor it.

A mortgage broker will be able to figure out how much you will be able to pay for a house. Once you know this, you will be set to work with a realtor to look around at some houses. A mortgage broker can also give you advice on finding a realtor, and can help direct you to a real estate lawyer, which you will need. Be sure to confirm that your mortgage broker, realtor, and lawyer are reputable. One often (though not always) reliable confirmation of reputability is how long someone has been providing their services (if they're doing shady things, they often can't last long. Word gets around, and law does come into play). Probably the best testimony of reputability is found in online reviews (just look them up).

Working with a Realtor

Before you contact a realtor, try to figure out exactly what you are looking for in a house, as well as everything that would be unacceptable. Though a realtor can help you with this process, it can take weeks of pondering and research before a clear vision of exactly what you want in a house begins to form. The realtor will try to quickly determine your wants, and if you haven't been considering them you will be approaching your house search with an uninformed and vague perspective. So take the time to think carefully about everything you want and don't want in a house and write it out in a list. If you aren't clear enough, you will end up wasting everyone's time by viewing houses which don't even meet your criteria. You might give your realtor a prepared list like this:

The House Must:

- be $420,000–$500,000
- be a bungalow
- be at least 1,500 square feet
- be move-in ready
- have a basement apartment suite
- have a double wide driveway
- have a garage
- have a dishwasher
- have central air conditioning
- be within a ten-minute drive to the office and train station
- be on a quiet two-lane residential street (not on a bus route)
- not be within a block of a rail line

The Dangerous "Starter Home" Concept

A "starter home" is a house that you can afford that will get you into home ownership as soon as possible. One which you fully intend to sell when you can afford a more expensive one. The concept of buying a house as a "starter home" only took traction in post-WW2 culture. When you are looking into buying your first house you would do well to steer clear of this relatively new and damaging mentality. There are a number of good reasons for this:

1. When you look at your house as a "starter home" you don't give it the chance to become a true home, one that you are content with. It becomes nothing more than a springboard to something better. This can foster an ungrateful attitude towards your home, and more broadly, your life (definitely a bad thing).

    I've heard many people complaining bitterly about their "starter homes" in which they feel trapped. Instead of being grateful for the roof over their heads, they are completely unsatisfied with the lack of north facing windows for instance, or something inconsequential like this. They are always pining for their "dream house."

2. As we will cover later, selling and then buying another house is an exceptionally expensive endeavor. Currently, there is on average an immediate $32,500 loss, plus the hassle of moving. This cost can set you back many years financially. So illusions of getting ahead financially by getting into the housing market a bit earlier can easily be swept away by these costs when you go to sell your house to buy another.

3. You may end up buying a house that you don't like, that needs lots of work, or is in a location you don't like, all with the thought that, "I'll only be here for a little while." Well, why subject yourself to all of that? Also, consider the possibility that you won't be able to make the move for one

reason or another. You will then be plagued with a house that does not suit you, and that is perhaps in need of many repairs that you can't tackle. Many people are in this situation. It's just not worth it.

Instead of looking at your first house as a "starter home," look at it as "my home." Should you end up moving, that will be a future concern. If this means that you have to save up a little more money, or take out a larger mortgage to get a house that you can be content with, it is absolutely worth it. Get a house that you like, that is built well, and is in a location that suits your lifestyle. Unless you are equipped financially, and are ready and able to do renovations, don't get a house that is in disrepair. That is to say, get a house that is "move-in ready."

Realize also that no one needs a giant house. A big house comes with big expenses, and requires more time to maintain. So consider buying a small or average-sized house. If you fear that your kids won't have enough room, consider that they can learn to live having to *share* space and *cooperate* more (desperately needed virtues in the world). A family of four can live quite comfortably in a 1,500-square-foot bungalow.

If you are able to find a good house that has a basement in-law suite, it is well worth paying $50,000 more for it. I strongly recommend owning an average-sized resale bungalow, with a basement suite that has a separate entrance, and space for tenant parking in the driveway.

Always get a home inspection from a reputable home inspector. The state of a house's foundation, furnace, plumbing, electrical wiring, windows, and roof are important considerations. Problems with these house systems may already be factored into the asking price, but you may not want to deal with them to begin with. Over time you can expect that things like your furnace and roof will need replacing, but a failing foundation is probably something you should simply steer clear of.

Making a Home Purchase and Finalizing Your Mortgage

When you have decided on a house to buy, you will work with your realtor to negotiate a final sale price with the seller. Once this has been agreed upon, your mortgage broker can work with you and a lender to sort out the best mortgage terms available to you. I have two suggestions for how to go about working out your mortgage terms:

1. Don't take an "adjustable-rate mortgage" (ARM) if you can get a traditional "fixed rate" mortgage, unless interest rates are exceptionally high. This is very important. Many people have been crushed financially by adjustable-rate mortgages.
2. Ensure that you are given good "prepayment privileges" in your mortgage terms. Your prepayment privileges should include options to make extra monthly payments, as well as lump sum payments towards the mortgage debt (the principal).

Pay Off Your Mortgage ASAP

Being mortgage free is a major financial milestone that will usher in a higher degree of financial independence and security in your life. There are many perks to being mortgage free, like high credit, freedom from large monthly mortgage payments, and a simplified financial life with fewer hassles.

Prepayment privileges allow you to make extra payments towards your mortgage debt so that you can save having to pay lots of interest while at the same time more quickly pay off your loan, and be mortgage free. You will be earning the equivalent of the interest rate of your loan (and it will be tax free interest) on the prepayments you make.

Note that mortgage interest rates are usually higher than those offered by savings accounts, bonds, or CDs which are also taxed. So, mortgage prepayments give you a relatively high and guaranteed return, and it's tax-free. This is why it is my opinion that extra mortgage payments are the best use of the money you can put towards your savings. Basically, if you owe money on your house, pay it off ASAP.

Get out of all the debt liability you are under and secure what is likely the most important financial asset in your life. Other investment and savings vehicles (which we will discuss later) can wait until your house is paid off. Basically, by making mortgage prepayments, you can use your house as a savings account that will pay you the interest saved on your mortgage loan as you more quickly approach the perks of being mortgage free.

An exception to prioritizing mortgage prepayments might be if you had the funds available to pay off your mortgage at any given time and could therefore utilize a low interest rate on a fixed rate mortgage, if such mortgage terms were available to you.

Some financial advisors recommend investing in the stock market before your house is paid off on the premise that the stock market has a good chance of profiting you more than the interest you would save by making prepayments. While this has many times been the case, especially when mortgage rates are very low, it certainly hasn't always. Many of the less tangible financial advantages of being mortgage free also get overlooked in the number crunching of these financial advisors.

Instead of looking at a low mortgage interest rate as a good excuse to invest money elsewhere, look at it as a window of opportunity to pay off your mortgage before you are forced to renew it at a possibly much higher interest rate. You want to minimize the time period over which you are inhibited by large monthly mortgage payments, debt liabilities, and insecurity in the ownership of your very home (something that is indeed worth securing).

Selling Your House and Buying Another

People decide to move from one house to another for various reasons: to upsize, to downsize, or perhaps to get a pay raise by moving from one city to another. Over the years I have noticed that many people are unaware of how much moving houses can cost. So let's go through a typical example to shed some light on this potential financial pitfall.

Suppose the sale price of your house is $420,000 (close to the national average at the time of the writing of this book).[17] Now, suppose that you are going to have to pay your realtor a 5.5% commission on that sale price. This will amount to about $21,000. Now add a land transfer tax of 2.15% or $8,500 for your new similarly priced home (this tax varies between 1-5% state-to-state). Now add legal fees of $1,000. Finally, add moving costs of $2,000 for a full house. Now add it all up:

$21,000 Realtor
 $8,500 Land Transfer Tax
 $1,000 Legal Fees
  $2,000 Moving Costs
$32,500 Total Cost

$32,500 is the total cost to move from one average house to another (plus the heaps of hassle and headaches involved with relocation).

So, you can see that selling your house to buy another one is a lot of money. In fact, the cost involved in this typical scenario will require most of an average person's full year's income to pay (after taxes). Unfortunately, the situation is even worse than it appears at this point.

Remember, "A dollar saved is *five* dollars earned." Well, that applies here as well. In order to *save* the roughly $30,000 needed to cover the expense of the house swap, you would have to *earn* roughly

$150,000. That's a lot of money, and therefore work, just to break even on the move. About two and a half years of average full-time work to be exact.

Had they known this, I think a lot of people would have saved a lot of loss and stress by avoiding an unnecessary move. Consider the case where the motivation to move comes from the offer of a pay raise. Suppose a $10,000 increase in annual salary is offered. Who wouldn't want that right? Well in this case the pay raise would take you about four and a half years just to break even on the move (after taxes on the $10,000).

Consider staying put and appreciating what you do have in your house and making it your *home* rather than a *hotel layover.* That is, unless you have a reason worthy of many years of full-time work to foot the bill. As is often said, "The grass always seems greener on the other side of the fence." Maybe it would be wise for us to stick to our side of the fence with what we know to be tried and true.

We can be grateful for our home and build a well-rooted life of contentment around it and our community rather than hopping all over the place. Forty years of wandering in the desert was not ideal for the nation of Israel. They were looking to permanently settle in the promised land of Canaan. If we are settled, we can work to stay, rather than sever everything to work.

That said, if you have a divine calling to a great opportunity to expand the fruitfulness of your life, as in the case of Abraham, a move will indeed be in order. Be aware of the cost however, and prayerful in your decision to move.

Buying a Second House as an Investment

Some people buy a second house as an investment (an income property). Home prices can certainly increase over time in a prospering region, while income can be obtained from rent. An income property can turn out to be a very good investment or a very bad one. This all depends on the price you pay for the property, the demand for it, and your ability to maintain and rent it wisely.

Real estate T.V. shows have given the term "income property" an alluring connotation. However, it is easy to become misinformed by the notion that income properties are passive income generators, allowing you to sit back and collect money without lifting a finger.

The truth is that an income property is a lot like many other small businesses. It involves many expenses and many hours of your time to manage. Your "profit" will probably feel a little more like your "pay" after the reality of income property ownership has set in. That is not to say that it isn't worth it to have an income property if the circumstances are fitting, just don't expect it to be a means of passive income.

Perhaps the most important factor of successful income property investment is in finding respectful and trustworthy tenants. Do everything you can to ensure that you are renting to good tenants. Enduring a vacancy for a time is a lot better than settling for bad tenants out of desperation.

Though it is not common (despite what you may hear), there certainly are some tenants who will refuse to pay rent once they have occupied your house, and then may cause physical damage to boot. That can be a very costly and stressful situation to find yourself in.

Here are a few insights into successful income property ownership:

1. Try to buy a house (or multiplex) for less than ten times its annual gross rent.
2. Having to hire repair and maintenance work to be done is exceptionally expensive. As I mentioned earlier, the mere replacement of a faucet can end up costing you $300 (not including the faucet!). Being handy and able to make repairs and keep up with maintenance work is a huge advantage to a

property owner and can even make or break your investment's profitability.

3. Do not think you can get away with being an absentee landlord (someone who never visits the property or corresponds with tenants). If you don't care about your property or tenants, your tenants won't care about you or your property. First of all, this means that your income property should be close to your home. It also means that you should be involved in maintenance, improvements, and talks with your tenants.

4. When you are interviewing prospective tenants, make it very clear that you are not an absentee landlord. Tell them that you will be by the property regularly to perform maintenance and to check on things. This will immediately ward off the worst of tenants who want nothing to do with astute landlords. The type of tenants that refuse to pay rent and trash up property want to have a landlord that doesn't come around much or know much about property ownership.

If you are handy, and home prices in your area are a good representation of value (as measured by the methods used earlier), then investing in an income property might be right for you. However, if there is good reason to believe that your area will not be prospering with growth in the years to come, or if home prices are unfavorably out of alignment with home values, stay away.

You should also realize that investing in an income property puts you in a position with little of the protection offered by diversification (as described later). Unless you are very wealthy, your income property will be one giant investment. Many of your eggs will be in that one basket. That said, around the globe and throughout history, income properties have often greatly benefited their owners. On the other hand, if you're not up for it, you may be better off investing in a way that does not demand too much of your time, and is flexible, like the stock market (which is covered in Part 4).

Part 4
Investing

Investing for God's Good Purposes

It is with some encouraging and cautionary Scripture that I want to enter the topic of investing.

As with many things, money can be used for good, or for evil. Throughout history the accumulation of wealth has been synonymous with greed. However, accrued wealth can also be a means to the fruitful works of God.

By way of fascinating circumstances, God brought Joseph to power in Egypt and used him not only to save his own family, but entire nations from destruction by famine (Genesis 37–50). With guidance from God, Joseph oversaw massive national investments in infrastructure to store excess agricultural produce. It was through the hoarding of large amounts of resources that great good was ultimately accomplished. Rather than the love of money, it was God's good purpose that motivated Joseph, who was perhaps the greatest investor of all time.

The parable of the rich fool, taught to us by Jesus (Luke 12:13–21), reveals the flip side to Joseph's approach to wealth management. Rather than God's good purpose, it was the love of wealth that motivated the rich fool to store up great excesses for *himself* and, when his life was taken, his excess grain may then have become the cause of quarreling among his sons or been wasted, not being used for any good (as is implied by the context of Luke 12:13–14). So Jesus blessedly warns us, "...Watch out! Be on your guard against all kinds of greed; a man's life does not consist in an abundance of his possessions" (Luke 12:15).

Automating Your Savings

As previously mentioned, a mortgage is one good way to "automate" your savings. Each month you must make a mortgage payment, and part of that payment goes towards growing the equity in your house. Eventually you will own your house in full. This is a type of *automatic*, or *forced*, savings. Automating your savings is a very effective way to successfully save money.[18] That is because when something is automatic it does not require special action to be taken, which often just doesn't happen.

Another way to automate your savings is to set up automatic monthly withdrawals from your bank account to be deposited into a savings account that you have set up to save and invest money. For instance, you can arrange with your bank to have $1,000 transferred monthly (a recurring contribution) into an appropriate savings account.

Earning Interest

You can earn interest on money by keeping it in an interest-bearing bank account, investing it in bonds, or certificates of deposit (CDs). The interest that bonds and CDs pay you is fixed at the time you purchase them. The allure of bonds and CDs is that they pay a fixed interest, so you don't have to worry about market fluctuations affecting your investment.

Though nothing is certain in this world, CDs and bonds offer a higher degree of certainty than other investments. This higher degree of certainty generally comes at the cost of a lower profit on your invested funds.

CDs and bonds are similar, but whereas bonds can be bought and sold at any time on an open market, CDs are held over a committed time period. Getting money out of a CD prematurely will cost you a penalty. It is this commitment to a time period of deposit with penalty that allows CDs to offer interest rates higher than most savings accounts.

Putting money into CDs or bonds likely won't be your best investment option if they are paying less than 5% in interest. In such a low interest market there is a good chance you would do better with money in the stock market or elsewhere. Note also that although interest gives you a return on invested money, it is taxed more than dividends (which we will discuss shortly). Suffice it to say that money can be made by collecting interest, and even more money can be made by compounding those gains by reinvesting them.

Compounding

In its first year, a sapling tree will only grow a few leaves. In its second year, maybe a dozen. In its twentieth year, however, it may add thousands of leaves and hundreds of pounds to its weight. As the tree gets bigger, it grows faster. If money did grow on trees it would be a perfect demonstration of the principle of compound interest (and also compound dividends).

In the same way that a tree grows, so will money by the process of compounding when you reinvest your earned interest or dividends (that is, when you use your payouts to increase the size of your investment).

As an example, suppose you were to double $1 twenty times. You would see it grow like this:

$2, $4, $8, $16, $32, $64, $128, $256, $512, $1,024, $2,048, $4,096, $8,192, $16,384, $32,768, $65,536, $131,072, $262,144, $524,288, $1,048,576

The first doubling would only gain $1, but the last doubling would gain over half a million dollars.

In a realistic investment scenario, if you were to invest $1,000, earning a 10% return annually, you would have about $6,700 after twenty years through the effect of compounding.

Tax Shelters and Tax Deferral

There is of course the matter of income tax to consider. Interest is taxed in the same way as your regular income. As mentioned earlier, one of the great advantages of making prepayments on your mortgage is that you earn the interest rate of your mortgage (usually higher than that offered by savings accounts, bonds, or CDs), and it will be tax free interest.

Profits from stock dividends, and capital gains from selling stock, investment real estate, or businesses are also taxed, but at a lower rate than regular income.

To understand the effects of income tax on investment profit, let's revisit the example of investing $1,000, earning 10% interest annually. Without any annual taxation, we saw that you would have about $6,700 after 20 years. However, paying 25% tax annually on your interest profits (the average income tax Americans paid in 2022), you would only have about $4,200 after that time. That's about 43% less profit.

Now let's look again at our example of investing $1,000, earning 10% interest annually, to see what would happen if we could defer taxation until the twenty years were over rather than paying tax annually. We saw that by paying tax annually we would have $4,200 (a gain of $3,200). We also saw that by paying no tax over the twenty-year period we would have $6,700 (a gain of $5,700, 43% more profit). Now, if we were to only pay tax after the twenty years we would have about $5,000 (That's 25% more money than had tax not been deferred).

One of the advantages of growing a business or owning stock or an investment property is that you only have to pay taxes at the time of the sale of these assets instead of on the gains you make each year. Not only will taxes on these investments be deferred, but your gains will be taxed at a much lower rate (capital gains tax) than normal income. The combination of tax deferral, and low capital gains tax can have an enormous effect on your profits.

Fortunately, there are ways to grow your investments (including interest yielding investments) using a tax-sheltered account like a 401k, IRA, or Tax-Deferred Annuity.

401ks and IRAs

Many employers offer a 401k retirement plan. Some will even match a percentage of your contributions as a payout. There is a good chance that using your employer's 401k plan will benefit you. You will be able to defer taxes by making contributions with income before it has been taxed. Within your 401k account you can make investments allowed by your employer.

Another great tax shelter for your retirement savings is an IRA (Individual Retirement Account). You can open an IRA yourself at most banks or brokerages, and there are often fewer limits to the investments that you can make within it than with a 401k.

You can use both a 401k and an IRA together. That way you can increase how much money you can contribute to your retirement savings (because there are yearly contribution limits for each type of account), as well as increase your investment options while possibly receiving payouts from your employer (if offered by your company's 401k plan).

Stocks and Dividends

Perhaps when you hear someone say "stock market" the first things that come to mind are "risk, crash, gambling, and loss." You wouldn't be alone in this. Many people think of investing in the stock market as mere irresponsible gambling.

Unfortunately, that belief is a costly misperception. A misperception that has its roots in a flawed understanding of the causes and outcomes of some of the financial tragedies of history. The foremost of the last century being "The Great Depression" when, beginning in 1929, a stock market "crash" saw the market lose almost 90% of its value over a three-year period. That's a lot of money that vanished into thin air.

For many people that financial cataclysm led to the blunt philosophy, "No stock market for me." But the truth is that it wasn't stocks, or the stock market, that was the problem at all. Rather, the problem was in how people were using them.

No one should have been buying stocks before the crash because they were ridiculously overpriced. Buying stock before that crash would have been like paying $100 for a sandwich in the hopes that you would be able to sell it to your uncle for $150 later at lunch. Likewise, no one should have sold their stocks when they subsequently became irrationally cheap following the crash.

Many stock market investors at the time were delusional with greed as stock prices shot up, and then blinded by irrational fear as stock prices fell down. It was all a matter of human emotion blundering in the absence of reason. Basically, many people did the polar opposite to that which was logical. Blinded by emotion, they bought high with elation and sold low with desolation. So you may ask, is the stock market nothing more than an emotional rollercoaster, then? The answer is no.

A stock is not a lottery ticket; it is a part-ownership of a business. That's right, when you buy stock in a company you take on an ownership stake in that company. Stock ownership has a far more concrete basis in business than many people realize, and that comes with the perks of business profit. As a business grows by making money, its value increases, and generally, so too will its stock.

Often, a business's profit will be used to further grow the business. Alternatively, part of the profit can be divided among shareholders and paid out to them. Such a payout is called a dividend. The amount of the dividend is usually described as the stock's *dividend-yield*, which is the percentage of the stock's price that is paid out each year. If you liked collecting dividends playing Monopoly as a kid, you may find it even more enjoyable using real money as an adult.

As a stock owner you are not merely holding a piece of paper to trade as its price fluctuates irrationally. You are a business owner who can patiently wait as the company grows and pays you dividends. Because of this, if you are going to buy stock, you should be committed to investing in the company over at least a three-year period. While there will be irrational fluctuations in stock price, if the company does well over time, this will generally be reflected in the stock price over the long term. As legendary investor Benjamin Graham observed, "In the short run, the market is a voting machine but in the long run it is a weighing machine."

Selecting Stocks and Using Stock Brokerages

To buy stocks you will need to use your 401k, or open a brokerage account where you can also open an IRA. Be warned that brokerage fees at traditional banks can be very expensive. I would recommend opening an account using a reputable online brokerage instead, where trading fees are minimal.

Stocks can be great investments, but the outcome will depend on the particular companies in which you buy stock, and the price you pay for these stocks. When I look for a company with good prospects as an investment, I ask a few key questions that most successful investors will consider:

1. **Is the company really important?** How easily would society function if the company were to stop operating? There are many businesses that, while making a profit, are simply not foundational to society in any way. With a slight economic shift here or there some companies can end up squashed. Stay away from these. Important, large companies that have been in business for a while are often called "blue chip" companies, and are often worth investing in.

2. **Does the company pay a dividend? If so, what is its yield?** I will only invest in dividend paying companies, and I aim for a 5% dividend-yield (although anything above 3% I will consider). Many successful stock investors will only invest in dividend paying stocks. As a cautionary note, dividend yields above 5% can be a sign of trouble with the company and are often not sustainable.

3. **Is the price of the stock a good deal?** You may after some consideration determine with certainty that a particular pair of shoes is of very high quality and therefore would be ideal to own. However, if the shoes are $5,000, you might be a fool to buy them. On the other hand, priced at $100 you would be a fool not to. Here, the poison is in the price, not the product. Such is the case with stocks.

   You need to consider the price you pay in relation to the earnings you get. This is called the "price per earnings ratio," or "PE," of the stock. If you pay $40 for a stock share that is earning $2 per year, then the PE is 20 (you are paying 20 times the yearly earnings). Generally speaking, you want to avoid stocks selling at PEs greater than 20. If you want a really good deal, keep an eye out for a PE below 15.

Many other factors are also important to assessing the value of a stock. These include reviewing balance sheets, annual statements, and considering operational history.

If you feel that you are not adequately informed to pick particular stocks (which includes most people), don't try to. Also, be careful not to blindly follow the advice of a friend. You can do very well (often better than professional investors) by investing in the stock market with Broad Index Funds, or Mutual Funds. These Funds offer a packaging of stocks from a number of companies that operate across various sectors of the economy (food, transportation, media, energy, communications, etc.).

Legendary investor Warren Buffett advises that individuals with little personal knowledge about stock investing can best benefit from the stock market by investing in an S&P 500 Index Fund ETF. It is important to note however that many prominent ETF providers use their large proxy voting rights to promote policies that are contrary to Christian values in the companies held in their funds. Consider instead Christian ETFs and Mutual Funds. Such funds will include dividend payouts and offer a healthy degree of diversification (see diversification).

Here is an example of an ideal investing scenario:

"I bought into a reputable Christian Mutual Fund and also bought shares of a reputable Christian ETF. I did this using an online stock brokerage in which I have an IRA set up. I also have CDs and some bonds in that account. My investment profits will grow tax free as I save up a down payment for a house."

Cash

The trouble with cash is that its buying power is eaten away over time by an insidious process known as inflation. We won't get into the reasons as to why inflation occurs. It is enough to know that inflation is a process by which a dollar loses its value over time.

It is illustrative to consider the fact that $1 in 1923 would buy almost $20 worth of goods today. Put in perspective, hourly wages were accordingly lower in 1923, so generally speaking you still had to work about as hard to get goods then as now. So, if you ever hear someone complaining about how expensive things are today by referencing a price from the past, keep in mind that they had to work a lot harder to get a dollar back then. Spoken with indignation, a statement like, "You could get a burger for one dollar when I was young!" is better understood in the context of, "I got paid just three dollars an hour when I was young!"

Inflation's value-eroding effect only becomes significant when you hold onto cash for an extended period. This makes cash like a hot potato, you will only get burned if you fail to pass it along into something of real value. Letting cash sit under your mattress or lay uninvested in your bank account submits it to decay. I knew of a couple who did just that and lost out big-time.

When we first moved to our neighborhood, a hard-working plumber who ran his own business gave me a ride in his truck. Speaking to me about retirement, he warned, "You don't want to end up eating cat food." Well, I certainly agreed with that.

After we had established our rather successful housing business, I was talking to his wife one day. Pointing out our tenanted properties she assured me to scorn that she would never do anything risky like that with their money. Nor would she risk their money in the stock market. She told me that they had agreed early on that she would be the one who would look after the money.

While her husband had wanted to invest in housing and the stock market, she had insisted that they do the responsible thing and save all the money from his many cash jobs as just that, cash, which they kept hidden away. She wasn't going to risk losing all that money, she proclaimed to me proudly.

I should point out here that it is never a good idea to put yourself in a scenario in which you present yourself as a desirable target for home robbery by divulging private financial information.

She may not have lost one red cent of that cash, but may have lost about half of its buying power over the years. The worst effect would have been on the money lying dormant the longest. In 1975, around the time my neighbor began his business, he may have been making a good hourly pay of $5 (minimum wage was $2.10 then). That saved $5 of cash, which at the time would have paid for a steak entree at a nice restaurant, will now get you little more than a coffee.

I went to that man's retirement party when he reached the milestone of 65. It was a joyful celebration, and everyone was glad to see that his back-breaking years had come to an end and that he could take things at his own pace. Sadly, a few years ago, I ran into him working around town for another company, at 75. It is not easy getting under a sink at that age.

Of course, all of this does not mean you should have no cash on hand. Having some cash readily available in your bank account (perhaps enough to cover a few months of living expenses) as well as a little bit on your person just makes sense.

Cryptocurrencies

There is a new means of transferring funds over the internet through a system that uses cryptocurrencies, like Bitcoin. You can exchange your dollars for Bitcoin, which can then be transacted electronically with the protection of encryption.

Bitcoin and other cryptocurrencies are anonymous, decentralized, and unregulated. Of course, all of these features make them an ideal means of hiding the financial transactions of criminal activity (money laundering). Many believe that this has been the major contributor to Bitcoin's success.

People who invested in Bitcoin early on made large profits. However, the gains Bitcoin investors enjoyed in the past could have easily been losses had governments decided to impose regulations. This can in fact happen at any time, upon which the value of cryptocurrencies would suddenly plummet.

Bitcoin does not fulfill any of the characteristics of a good investment because it in no way embodies or produces any real value whatsoever. Investing in cryptocurrencies like Bitcoin is therefore not a well-informed financial decision, but rather a blind gamble (as Warren Buffett frequently points out).[19]

A currency not backed by anything tangible is like a pyramid scheme. Both are held up entirely by trust. As more people want to put their money into the currency, it trades at a higher price. As with a pyramid scheme, however, there is no real value present, only demand. This creates an unpredictable situation that will fall apart rapidly as soon as investors get spooked. So, while Bitcoin may indeed leap in price in the future, it may also plummet to zero. There is no good reason to expect anything because there is no foundation of actual value, only demand from all the hype emanating from its proponents.

Whether "crypto" or "paper", currencies should not be looked to as a means of protecting or creating value, but as a means of transacting value. If we are to take hold of our God given dominion on earth and build real things, we should not hoard wealth in a mere currency, crypto or otherwise. We should seek to create and steward real assets, like businesses, homes, and resources for those in need. Real estate and business assets are immune to currency fluctuations because they are real things of value, not just scales that weigh things of value (you can own business assets by owning a business or stock shares of one).

Currencies rise and fall on the whims of policy makers. Hold value in real assets, and look at currencies of all types as hot potatoes.

Precious Metals

Precious metals like gold and silver can be other vehicles in which to harbor some of your wealth. Precious metals have been known to protect wealth from the value-eroding effect of inflation described earlier, and they also protect funds from other financial calamities. Owning some also helps you to achieve a healthy degree of diversification (covered next).

Historically, gold has carried its value very well. Currencies have risen and fallen, but an ounce of gold has almost always held strong. It wouldn't hurt to hold about 5% to 10% of your wealth in gold. It should be noted here that silver has had a much more erratic track record and can also be more expensive to transact, so I would recommend gold as the precious metal of choice.

Diversification

We've all heard this one before: "Don't put all of your eggs in one basket." Spreading your eggs between different baskets to reduce the risk of a single large loss is the basis of financial diversification.

There are many ways in which you can spread your wealth to achieve diversification. Here is a list of scenarios progressing from no diversification to a healthy degree of diversification:

- Invest all of your savings in a house (a good first step)
- Split your savings between a house and an Index Fund

- Split your savings between a house, an Index Fund, and gold
- Split your savings between a house, an Index Fund at brokerage A, a different Index Fund at brokerage B, gold, and cash in the bank

The practice of diversification can be justifiably delayed until your house is paid off. The benefits and importance of home ownership overshadow the advantages of diversification. If you've been straddling your mortgage along for a drawn-out period while playing financial acrobatics elsewhere, you may find yourself unable to make monthly payments or refinance at a higher interest rate if the stock market takes a hit and you lose your job (these things often go hand in hand). Perhaps you could have paid off your mortgage a decade earlier, freeing up large monthly sums to invest while having the security of your home. Try to secure your house first.

Annuities

An annuity is a financial arrangement you can set up that provides you with a guaranteed regular income. It is purchased with your savings to help simplify and secure your finances, usually in your retirement years. You wouldn't normally buy an annuity until you have retired, if at all, but it would be worthwhile to consider the option, perhaps talking it over with a financial advisor a few years before you plan to retire.

The regular payments you receive from an annuity are a combination of:

1. Interest earned on the money you have paid to purchase it.
2. A gradual return of the money you have paid (the capital).

3. Money from annuity holders who die earlier than expected (which is transferred to those who live longer than expected).

As you can see, as well as simplifying your finances, annuities also act as a kind of retirement-income insurance policy. If you end up living longer than average, a *life-annuity* will cover those later years of your life indefinitely. You can buy annuities from many insurance companies.

You can also set up a tax-deferred annuity in a 401k or IRA account as a means to save for retirement. You could pay into it to save for retirement, deferring taxes until you start receiving your regular payments. That is, your contributions are made with income that is not taxed.

If you have a good pension plan and are willing and able to manage your own money, annuities may not be a good option. An annuity places a large amount of your net worth in the trust of a single basket. For this reason I would suggest you not put your entire savings into an annuity. There are also fees that must be paid with annuities, as well as penalties if you need to withdraw your money from them early. Also, if you die earlier than expected, your estate can end up losing money.

If you own your house mortgage-free, and have some other pension income, buying an annuity with your savings might make sense if you would prefer not to manage them yourself. The annuity would be a part of your diversified investment portfolio.

A Plan to Save Money for a Down Payment

If you want to become a homeowner, you will need a plan of action to save money for the down payment and the other costs involved in a home purchase. Yet many people never get serious about forming and committing to a plan of action. The following is an example of a simple and sensible plan of action that can be used to build up the needed savings to get you into homeownership:

Suppose that you have made it your aim to purchase a house for $400,000 within two years time (you will never know what the future holds for house prices, but you must have a goal). In this case you will need:

1. At least $12,000 for the down payment (3% of the home price).
2. At least $10,000 for the other expenses involved in the house purchase. Called closing costs, these include land transfer tax, legal fees, moving costs, and a number of smaller expenses.
3. At least $10,000 in additional savings to cover your bills coming due, unexpected stuff, and a few months of living expenses should you need it.
4. An extra $5,000 for good measure, because the first three points mentioned above are "at least" statements.

Therefore, you will be looking to reach a total savings of $37,000 over the next two years. If you currently have $10,000 saved as cash in the bank, you will need to save an additional $27,000 to achieve your goal. Here's the plan:

1. Pay off your debts. First and foremost, your credit cards.
2. Earn more money by taking on some extra work if possible.
3. Don't get sucked into drive-throughs for expensive fast-food. Other unnecessary expenses should also be curtailed. Avoid cool cars.
4. To meet all of your banking needs, and to hold your $10,000 of back-up cash, consider using a bank that does not charge monthly banking fees and that pays out some interest on the money you have deposited.
5. Open an online brokerage account at a reputable online brokerage.

6. Set up an IRA within your brokerage account.

7. Set up monthly recurring contributions of up to $540 to be transferred automatically from your bank into your IRA, ensuring that you maintain a $10,000 cash reserve at your bank, and that you do not over-contribute ($540 is based on the 2023 allowance).

8. Every month or two, with the money deposited into your IRA, purchase shares of a reputable Christian ETF, or buy into a Christian mutual fund, CDs, or bonds.

9. To realize the benefit of diversification you may want to spread your funds between ETFs, mutual funds, CDs, and bonds.

10. Keep saving, investing, and profiting *tax free* until you reach your goal. When you become a homeowner, start using your house as the next place in which to grow your savings. Your recurring savings contributions will become your monthly mortgage payments and the mortgage prepayments that you will make (with as high a frequency as you can manage).

This approach bolsters hope, sets a defined goal, and gives you a plan to achieve it. Without a concrete plan, you may not get very far saving money to purchase a house.

Unfortunately, as with everything else earthly, there are no certainties in the financial world. Though many people believe they will find total security in their cash by investing in nothing, the effect of inflation, which at times can be crippling, suggests otherwise. Though a reputable ETF or mutual fund is usually a good investment, there can always be downturns in the stock market from time to time. If such a downturn occurs you need to be patient and continue on with your regular incremental purchases. If you panic and sell at a loss, or if you are uncomfortable at the idea of a market downturn, it may be best for you to stick with CDs and bonds going forward. You will likely earn less profit, but you will be able to sleep at night and won't be losing money by selling at the worst time.

An Eye-Opening Financial Exercise

Suppose you buy a new couch for $2,000, instead of giving your old one a make-over by putting a cover over it to hide the stains.

a) Considering that "a dollar saved is X dollars earned", how much you will have to earn to cover this unnecessary expense?

b) Were you to have put that $2,000 towards a mortgage prepayment instead, how much will it have profited you by the time your mortgage is paid off? Assume a 5% interest rate, 2.5% inflation, and a 30-year amortization. Use an online interest calculator if needed.

c) Taken together (the required earnings, plus the lost potential savings of interest), how much did you actually spend on the unnecessary couch?

Answers

a) You paid $2,000 for the couch. If X = 5 for you, $2,000 will be all you can accumulate from $10,000 of your earnings.

b) You put the $2,000 towards a prepayment on your mortgage. At an interest rate of 5%, minus an average inflation of 2.5%, you will profit by 2.5% annually, compounded over 30 years, $2,000 will yield $2,200 in profit (the amount above the $2,000 initial investment).

c) Overall, if you buy the couch, you will effectively lose $10,000 worth of progress from your employment, while at the same time lose $2,200 worth of potential progress from interest savings on your mortgage. Therefore, the couch will ultimately cost you an amazing $12,200. That's more than six times the nominal cost!

Part 5
Making It on Your Own

Starting A Business

As is often said, "nothing ventured, nothing gained." This world owes much of its prosperity to those who, by the grace of God, ventured to start their own business and created something of value. These people accepted God's offering of dominion of the earth. However, an entrepreneur must proceed with wisdom, hard work, and caution. Passion will serve very well too, but if it is out of alignment with reality it can cause costly damage.

Starting your own business can be fulfilling, freeing, and profitable. Or it can be the opposite of all those things. If you are very emotional, impulsive, lack organizational skills, or lack logical reasoning skills (i.e., math), you will likely find yourself overwhelmed and eventually bankrupt in business. I've seen this play out before.

Though Hollywood would surely disagree, I would hazard this business advice: Do not simply follow your heart blindly. In reality, our hearts can lead us straight to ruin (Jeremiah 17:9; Proverbs 19:3). Do, however, follow God's direction and pray for guidance.

Oftentimes people create a dream business in their mind. They start to build a fantasy that includes everything they want. Enchanted by this fantasy, they try to bring it into reality. Reality will often not bear our fantasies, however.

I remember a woman who wanted nothing more than to provide a wholesome "hang-out" venue for the teenagers in her small town. This was in fact a very admirable goal, and may have worked in other circumstances. As it was, she tried to grow the seed of her dream business using her own light, rather than the light of the truth.

She must have envisioned a bustling teen stomping ground. There was going to be a pool table, couches, milk shakes and snack food for sale, and a jukebox. She got merchandise made that she featured in a display case; duffle bags, mugs, and the like, all with her business logo on them. She was so worried that she would be overwhelmed with customers that she had two cash registers staffed and ready to go on opening day. Opening day came, but teens didn't.

What was the problem? First, the town was so small that there were hardly any teens to start with. Second, she set up her establishment in an out of the way place on the outskirts of the town that had no curb appeal. It had almost no customer base, little allure, was poorly marketed, and was awkward to get to. On the grand opening day, in an empty little 200-square-foot space, two cashiers awaited customers in awkward silence.

Visiting again a few months later, it was the same story. In the silent void of the venue, a cashier waited listlessly. The owner came out to speak to my wife and I eagerly. "How can we get more kids to come?" she asked us. She had not realized that her dream could not come to fruition in that town and location. Sadly, she was likely running things at a loss and keeping it all afloat with her savings. Talking with her, it was clear that she was not equipped with the skills to run a business. Many of the decisions she was making were financially irrational. She was a kind woman with good intentions, but she did not have the skills or mindset to run a business successfully.

Before you start a business, ask yourself, do you have the knowledge, skill, and temperament to run a business? If you cringe at the thought of basic math, that is an ominous foreshadowing of a shuttered business. However, if you are skilled and passionate about something that many people want, you may be able to start a business that prospers for years to come.

It would be worth considering how much demand exists for the product or service you are looking to offer. Are people going to be willing to pay money for it? Also note that some industries are inherently difficult to profit in. This includes the restaurant industry for instance, in which businesses have a notoriously high rate of failure. That doesn't mean that you will not succeed, but it would be foolish to overlook the fact that many hard-working people have lost everything in such ventures. God continually beseeches us to act with wisdom and avoid following our unbridled passions, as compelling as they can be.

In the least, you should be comfortable with simple finance and math going into a business endeavor. Consider seeking some business education before you get too serious about starting your own venture. This does not mean that you have to spend years of your life training at a college or university. Get yourself an introductory textbook on small business management and study it independently. This alone will give you a huge edge over many others who are starting small businesses blindly.

Avoiding Scams

So far, we have gone over how we can end up scamming *ourselves* financially. Unfortunately, there are others out there who will try to scam us as well. Remember, "A fool and his money are soon parted." If someone has called or emailed you asking for personal information, do not give them any. If they are associated with your bank, they will know any needed personal information already. To be certain, call your bank yourself and ask if they need to speak with you.

I remember how a neighbor to one of our income properties was always being scammed. In fact, the very first time we talked he plainly told me that he was easy to scam. I was amazed that he said that to me. He hardly knew me! He went on to describe a number of times he had fallen victim to trickery. One day he pulled me aside and triumphantly explained that he was now protected from scammers. A company offering to protect all of his online accounts from hacking had called him. All he had to do, he explained, was to pay a small monthly fee and give them all his passwords and personal information!

Don't give out your personal information and passwords. Scammers have a way of making it seem like their request for information is a valid exception, but don't be fooled. If someone has contacted you by phone or email and has got you feeling afraid, or you feel a sense of urgency, there is a very good chance that you are being led into a trap. Scammers use the power of fear to guide their victims into their clutches.

If someone comes to you promoting an investment, it is probably best to stay away. In the least, ask yourself these questions before getting into a solicited investment:

1. Are the promoters trustworthy? Look them up online.
2. The venture they are promoting will involve an underwriter, auditor, and legal firm. Are they trustworthy? Look them up. If it's a fly-by-night operation these parties will be small, perhaps a single person, and will not have established a good reputation.
3. Who is the regulator? What region is the venture registered in? Fly-by-nights will often be run from poorly regulated countries.
4. Is a huge pay-off being promised? If it sounds to good to be true … you know.
5. Are the promoters trying to instill a sense of urgency? If so, stop communicating with them.

If in doubt, seek consultation from a financial advisor before making a large investment.

Finally, I want to point out that it is never a good idea to volunteer information that will leave you vulnerable. I was once at a garage sale and the homeowner asked me if there was anything in particular that I was looking for. Jokingly, I said that I was looking for gold. In all seriousness he told me he had lots of gold in his house in a box, "fine Italian gold," he assured me. He didn't seem to be looking to sell it, but was just boasting of his fine gold. He implied that he would go in and bring it out just to prove to me that he had lots of gold. I indicated that that would not be necessary. This nice old man seemed to be just asking for a break-and-enter.

Part 6
Summary

Summary of Key Financial Concepts

1. We are exhorted by Jesus to give to our heart's content, and having been saved by grace, our heart's content will be found in giving.

2. Remind yourself that "a dollar saved is *five* dollars earned" each time you reach for your wallet.

3. "A fool and his money are soon parted." Identify your "expensive tastes" and get rid of them.

4. Ensuring that our time and money don't go unnecessarily to those who don't really need them is a good way to follow our Lord. We should try to direct our resources into the hands of loving stewards of the fruits of our labor.

5. "If it ain't broke, don't fix it." Be careful when considering an expensive home renovation/remodeling. Do-It-Yourself, "DIY," is a good option when a task is within your capability to complete. Don't skimp on the cost of building materials and hired labor. You want to "do it right the first time."

6. "Cars keep the poor, poor"... unless you spend carefully. Buy a used car. Choose a make/model that is proven to be

reliable. Own it without a loan if possible. Buy a "cool bumper sticker" instead of a "cool car." It's a lot cheaper.

7. Whether it be with your home, car, or clothes, if you want to stay "fashionable" you may find yourself "fashionably late" in owning your house or securing anything of worthy substance.

8. Don't waste food. Cut back on restaurant dining and drive-thrus. Focus on cheap but healthy foods rather than expensive snacks and alcohol. Flyers and coupons can be a great way to save money, but be sure to avoid being lured into unnecessary purchases and grocery store trips. Cross reference unit prices, check expiry dates, and go to bulk stores for items that you use frequently. Also, a chest freezer may be worth investing in, depending on your particular household and habits.

9. Using low-flow shower heads, replacing old toilets (pre-1992), and installing sufficient attic insulation and proper door weather-stripping will probably end up saving you more than you spend in the effort.

    The installation of an electric hot water tank timer could automatically save you over $3,000 over 20 years. An insulating jacket for your tank will also offer a good payback.

    Keep in mind that you may never break even on some of the more expensive upgrades to the energy efficiency of a house (like new windows and solar panels), or it might take decades.

10. If you have an older working appliance, not only might its replacement with a new energy efficient appliance end up costing you more money than it saves, but it may also end up using more energy than it saves. The claim of "energy saving" can in fact end up being "pocket draining."

11. In my experience there is no better way to put together your wardrobe than shopping at thrift stores. You will often find brand new clothing at a third of the cost or less. The selection at some of these stores can also be extensive because rarely are any two garments alike. Therefore, in a single shopping trip you may be able to fulfill a lot of your clothing needs, sidestepping the hassle of running around town to multiple stores.

12. Be careful when it comes to "sales." Remember the Swedish proverb, "If you buy what you don't need, you steal from yourself." The way I think of it, if something is on sale for 50% off, it is 100% too much money if you don't need it. Sales tend to bend our rational thinking and can lead to unneeded purchases and other costly behaviors. So, ask yourself the questions, "Do I really need this?" and, "Haven't I lived well enough without it?" Another good idea would be to sleep on it before making a decision.

13. Be a dollar pincher rather than a penny pincher. Make the most of money, but not by wasting your time worrying away trying to save a few cents. Ballpark prices a bit, saving a dollar here and a dollar there, keeping a watchful eye on things while not obsessing about negligible amounts.

14. Don't be "penny wise, but pound foolish." Don't miss the forest for the trees. Even if you can get those pennies clear in your focus, you'd be better off zooming out to look at the things that will have a larger impact on your finances. This folly happens all the time when people indiscriminately hire the company that gives them the cheapest possible quote to do work on their house. They may save $1,500 on a $10,000 job, but then have to pay for the $10,000 job all over again in a

97

year. Pay a little more if it will mean you can "do it right the first time."

15.   Stick to quality goods and services, remembering that "if it sounds too good to be true, then it probably is." Use online reviews and advice from friends to get a good sense of the true quality of a product. The most important thing you can do before making a purchase is to verify that you will be buying a reliable product.

16.   Buy quality goods used. Online marketplaces are easily searchable with huge stock available, so you can effectively track down what you need at a fraction of the retail price, and in a fraction of the time. You also won't get sidetracked by things you are not actually looking for.

While garage sales and thrift stores may be good places to find deals, you are shopping around blind, not knowing what the stock will hold (an exception is thrift store clothing which is usually well stocked and worth looking through). Also, unnecessary purchases are often made at garage sales and thrift stores.

You can save thousands on needed furniture, appliances, and tools in just a few minutes by sleuthing around the online marketplace for used goods when needed.

17.   I recommend making a budget, if only to acquaint yourself more fully with your financial activity and alleviate stress. While budgets can be very useful, they are not absolutely imperative to financial success. So do not give up if you are stubbornly unwilling to keep one. No budget can help you manage your necessary expenses because you simply can't avoid them. With what remains after those necessary expenses are paid, if you simply follow sound principles of financial wisdom, you will do as well with or without a detailed budget.

That said, sound principles of financial wisdom are easy to lose sight of without a budget.

18.   Real estate gives you a *real estate,* and not just a promise on a note of paper. You can live in a house, and everyone needs to live somewhere. This makes a house likely the best asset you will own and therefore a reliable and worthy place to invest money.

19.   Buying a house with the help of a mortgage will set you up with a routine of forced monthly payments. Unlike rent, monthly mortgage payments create a good routine of forced monthly savings.

20.   If things go south, you may be very glad you got a house with a basement suite that you can rent to a tenant.

21.   If you haven't saved enough for retirement, or if times get tough, you can always borrow money from your house. One way of doing this is through a reverse mortgage. Another way is through a line of credit with a bank.

22.   A mortgage broker's job is to serve you, not the banks, so ideally, they will be on your side, finding you a lender and helping you work out the best terms for your mortgage contract. The services of a reputable independent mortgage broker will be well worth the fee.

23.   Try to figure out specifically what it is you are looking for in a house before you contact a realtor. Then, make sure that your realtor knows exactly what you are looking for, as well as everything that would be unacceptable to you. The best way to be prepared ahead of time is with a list (see page 56). If you

aren't clear enough, you will end up wasting everyone's time by viewing houses which don't meet your criteria.

24.   Avoid the dangerous "starter home" concept. Here are three reasons why: 1. When you look at your house as a "starter home" you don't give it the chance to become a true home that you are content with. It becomes nothing more than a springboard to something better. This can foster an ungrateful attitude towards your home, and more broadly, your life. 2. Selling and then buying another house is an exceptionally expensive endeavor. Illusions of getting ahead financially by getting into the housing market a bit earlier can easily be swept away by these costs when you go to sell and buy another house. 3. You may folly into buying a house that you don't like, that needs lots of work, or is in a location you don't like. Consider the possibility that you won't be able to make the move to your dream house for one reason or another.

Instead of looking at your first house as a "starter home," consider looking at it as "my home." If this means that you have to save up a little more money, or take out a larger mortgage to get a house that you can be content with, it is absolutely worth it. Realize also that no one needs a giant house. Get one that you like that is built well and in a location that works for you. Unless you are equipped financially, and are ready and able to complete renovations, don't get a house that is in serious disrepair. That is to say, get a house that is "move-in ready."

25.   A family of four can live quite comfortably in a 1,500-squarefoot bungalow. If you are able to find a good house that has a basement suite, it is well worth paying $50,000 more for it than for a similar house without one. I strongly recommend looking for an average-sized resale bungalow with a basement

bachelor suite that has a separate entrance and space for tenant parking in the driveway.

26. Always get a home inspection from a reputable home inspector before committing to a house purchase.

27. When you work out your mortgage terms, don't agree to an "adjustable-rate mortgage" (ARM) if you can get a traditional "fixed rate" mortgage, unless interest rates are exceptionally high. This is very important. Many people have been crushed financially by adjustable-rate mortgages. Ensure that you are given good "prepayment privileges" in your mortgage terms. Your prepayment privileges should include options to make extra monthly payments, as well as lump sum payments towards the mortgage debt (the principal). It is my opinion that mortgage prepayments are the best possible use of the money that you can put towards savings.

28. Selling your house and buying another is surprisingly expensive. If you're in an average house and have an average income, in order to *save* the roughly $30,000 needed to cover the expense of the house swap, you may have to *earn* roughly $150,000. Consider staying put and appreciating what you do have in your house, making it your *home* rather than a *hotel layover*. Try building a rooted life of contentment around your home instead of rebuilding a home every time life changes.

29. Automating your savings is a very effective way to successfully save money. That is because when something is automatic it does not require special action to be taken, which often just doesn't happen. You can set up monthly automatic withdrawals from your bank account to be deposited into a savings account that you have set up to save and invest money.

30.   CDs (Certificates of Deposit) and bonds pay you interest on the money you invest into them. They pay a fixed interest so you don't have to worry about market fluctuations affecting them. Putting money into CDs or bonds likely won't be your best investment option if they are paying less than 5% in interest, however.

31.   As a tree gets bigger, it grows faster. If money did grow on trees it would be a perfect illustration of the principle of compounding. Interest or dividends collected from investments will compound in the same way that a tree grows if you keep reinvesting your profits.

32.   Interest is taxed in the same way as your regular income. As mentioned earlier, one of the great advantages of making prepayments on your mortgage is that you will earn the interest rate of your mortgage, and it will be tax free interest (and likely be at a higher rate than CDs or bonds).

        One of the advantages of growing a business or owning an investment property is that you only have to pay taxes at the time of the sale of these assets instead of on the gains you make each year on them. Not only will taxes on these investments be deferred, but your gains will be taxed at a much lower rate than normal income. The combination of tax deferral, and low capital gains tax can have an enormous effect on your profits.

33.   Many employers offer a 401k retirement plan. Some will even match a percentage of your contributions as a payout. There is a good chance that using your employer's 401k plan will benefit you. Another great tax shelter for your retirement savings is an IRA (Individual Retirement Account). You can open an IRA yourself at most banks or brokerages, and there are often fewer limits to the investments that you can make

within it than with a 401k. You can use both a 401k and an IRA together. That way you can increase how much money you can contribute to your retirement savings (because there are yearly contribution limits for each type of account).

34.   As a stockholder, you are a business owner, and that comes with the perks of business profit. If the business you have a share in grows, its value increases, and generally, so too will your stock's value. Often, the business's profit will be used to grow the company. Alternatively, part of the profit can be divided among shareholders and paid out as a dividend.

35.   If you feel that you are not adequately informed to select particular stocks, you can invest in a broad Index Fund such as a reputable Christian ETF. Such a broad Index Fund is a sampling of the market as a whole. You could also buy into a Christian mutual fund. These investments will include dividend payouts and inherently offer a healthy degree of diversification. You can invest by using a reputable online stock brokerage in which you can set up an IRA to shelter your investments from taxation.

36.   The problem with letting cash sit under your mattress, or lay uninvested in your bank account, is that its buying power can be eaten away by inflation. Consider that $10 back in 1923 could have bought you a nice new bike. However, it is a good idea to have enough cash in the bank to cover a few months of living expenses.

37.   Unless you are simply using it for a brief financial transaction, steer clear of cryptocurrency. Investing long-term in cryptocurrencies like Bitcoin is not a well-informed decision. Whether "crypto" or "paper", currencies should not be looked to as a means of protecting or creating value, but as a means

of transacting value (which is all they are). Currencies rise and fall on the whims of policy makers. Hold value in real assets, and look at currencies of all types as hot potatoes.

38.   Precious metals have been known to protect against inflation and economic downturns. Historically, currencies have come and gone, but an ounce of gold has almost always held strong. Silver has had a more erratic track record than gold and can be more expensive to transact.

39.   "Don't put all of your eggs in one basket." Spreading your eggs between different baskets in order to reduce the risk of a single large loss is the basis of financial diversification. To achieve diversification you might split your savings between a house, an Index Fund at brokerage A, a different Index Fund at brokerage B, gold, and cash in the bank. As an exception, diversification is something that can wait until your house is paid off.

40.   An annuity is a financial arrangement you can set up that provides you with a guaranteed regular income. You wouldn't normally buy an annuity with your savings until you have retired, if at all. As well as simplifying your finances, annuities also act as a kind of retirement-income insurance policy. If you end up living longer than average, a "life-annuity" will cover those later years of your life indefinitely. You can buy annuities from some insurance companies.

41.   Starting your own business can be fulfilling, freeing, and profitable. Or it can be the opposite of all those things. If you are very emotional, impulsive, or lack logical reasoning skills (i.e. math skills) you will likely find yourself overwhelmed and eventually bankrupt in business.

42.   Seek some basic small business education before you get too serious about starting a business venture. Simply getting an introductory textbook on small business and studying it independently will give you a huge advantage over many others who are starting their small businesses blindly.

Though Hollywood would surely disagree, I would hazard this business advice: Do not simply follow your heart blindly. In reality, our hearts can lead us straight to ruin. Do, however, follow God's direction and pray for guidance.

If nothing is ventured, nothing is gained. Starting a business can lead to a great career and a great contribution to society as well. Be careful however, work hard, and proceed with a reasonable disposition.

43.   Remember, "A fool and his money are soon parted." If someone has called or emailed you asking for personal information, do not speak to them. Anyone from your bank will know your personal information already. To be certain, call your bank yourself and ask if they need to speak with you. Scammers strive to make it seem like their correspondence is urgent and important. Be aware of this and don't be fooled. If you feel frightened, there is a good chance that you are being led into a trap. Fear is a primary tool that scammers use to their advantage.

Be very cautious of promoters trying to solicit your investment. Also, do not volunteer personal financial information.

The Most Important Financial Lessons all in One Page

Seek joy in the Lord, and in the people in your life, places where it can be found. It will never be found in *things*. The ticket to happiness is love, given freely by Jesus Christ. We are exhorted by Jesus to give to our heart's content, and having been saved by grace, our heart's content will be found in giving.

If you have an average job, most of your earnings end up going towards basic living expenses. For most of us, a dollar will only be available to save after five dollars have been earned. That is, "A dollar saved is *five* dollars earned." In fact, a dollar saved is like the cream skimmed off the top of your earnings.

Mortgage interest rates are usually higher than those offered by savings accounts, bonds, or CDs, which are also taxed. So, mortgage prepayments give you a relatively high and guaranteed return, and it's tax-free. This is why it is my opinion that extra mortgage payments are the best use of the money you can put towards your savings. Basically, if you owe money on your house, pay it off ASAP.

One of the advantages of growing a business or owning stock or an investment property is that you only have to pay taxes at the time of the sale of these assets instead of on the gains you make each year. Not only will taxes on these investments be deferred, but your gains will be taxed at a much lower rate (capital gains tax) than normal income. The combination of tax deferral, and low capital gains tax can have an enormous effect on your profits.

If you feel that you are not adequately informed to pick particular stocks (which includes most people), don't try to. Also, be careful not to blindly follow the advice of a friend. You can do very well (often better than professional investors) by investing in the stock market with Broad Index Funds, or Mutual Funds.

List of Helpful Financial Quotes and Sayings

From Scripture:

1. Honor the Lord with your wealth, with the first fruits of all your crops (Proverbs 3:9).
2. Lazy hands make a man poor, but diligent hands bring wealth (Proverbs 10:4).
3. The plans of the diligent lead to profit as surely as haste leads to poverty (Proverbs 21:5).
4. A generous man will himself be blessed, for he shares his food with the poor (Proverbs 22:9).
5. Do not be anxious about anything, but in everything, by prayer and petition, with thanksgiving, present your requests to God … (Philippians 4:6).

Old Adages:

1. A fool and his money are soon parted.
2. Give a man a fish and he will eat for a day. Teach a man to fish and he will eat for a lifetime.
3. The grass always seems greener on the other side of the fence.
4. The best things in life are free.
5. Spending is quick, earning is slow.
6. If you buy what you don't need, you steal from yourself.
7. Don't be penny wise, but pound foolish.
8. Don't try to keep up with the Joneses.
9. If it ain't broke, don't fix it.
10. The rich get richer.
11. It takes money to make money.
12. Interest grows without rain.
13. If it sounds too good to be true, then it probably is.
14. Do it right the first time.

15. You get what you pay for.
16. Avoid debt like the plague.
17. Nothing ventured, nothing gained.

From the Author:

1. A dollar saved is *five* dollars earned.
2. *Disposable* income is better viewed as *savable* income.
3. Seek joy in the Lord, and in the people in your life, places where it can be found. It will never be found in *things*.
4. Buy a cool bumper sticker instead of a cool car. It's a lot cheaper.
5. If you want to stay 'fashionable' you may find yourself 'fashionably late' owning your house.
6. Expensive tastes would be best nipped in the taste bud.
7. 50% off is 100% too much money for an unneeded item.
8. Just jog to your gym and back instead of paying for a membership there. It's a lot cheaper.
9. Often those that float around in their early years doing whatever they want in the process of *finding* themselves, end up completely *losing* themselves.
10. Buy a 'my home,' not a 'starter home.'
11. Sound principles of financial wisdom are easy to lose sight of without a budget.
12. Ask yourself, "Do I really need this?" and "Haven't I lived well enough without it?"
13. The ticket to happiness is love, given freely by Jesus Christ.

Notes

1. Thomas Sowell, *Social Justice Fallacies* (Basic Books, 2023), p. 108-109.

2. Ramsey, 20 December 2023 *ramseysolutions.com, What are the Average American's Monthly expenses?* Accessed 15 March 2024 <https://www.ramseysolutions.com/budgeting/american-average-monthly-expenses>

3. H&R Block *Tax Calculator* Accessed 15 March 2024 < https://www.hrblock.com/tax-calculator/>

4. Whitney Vandiver, and Shannon Bradley, 29 February 2024 *nerdwallet.com, What is the Total Cost of Owning a Car?* Accessed 15 March 2024 <https://www.nerdwallet.com/article/loans/auto-loans/total-cost-owning-car>

5. Jeff S. Bartlett, 13 September 2023 *Consumerreports.org, Cars are Expensive. Here's why and what You can do About it.* Accessed 15 March 2024 <https://www.consumerreports.org/cars/buying-a-car/people-spending-more-on-new-cars-but-prices-not-necessarily-rising-a3134608893/>

6. Justin Pritchard and MoneySense editors, 30 June 2023
   MoneySense, Toyota Corolla review: The Best Used Small Sedan For 2023
   Accessed 21 October 2023
   <https://www.moneysense.ca/spend/shopping/auto/toyota-corolla-review-the-best-used-small-sedan/>

7. USDA Food and Nutrition Service, U.S. Department of Agriculture, 2023

8. Lance Stevens, 14 November 2023
   Gallop Blog, Helping America Solve Its Food Wast Problem.
   Accessed 16 March 2024
   <https://news.gallup.com/opinion/gallup/513977/helping-america-solve-food-waste-problem.aspx>

9. DoxoINSIGHTS, 2023
   U.S. Utilities Market Size and Household Spending Report
   Accessed 16 March 2024
   <https://www.doxo.com/wp-content/uploads/2024/01/United-States-2023-Utilities-Industry-Household-Spending-doxo-insights-Report.pdf?utm_source=insights>

10. EPA, Office Of Water, Washington D.C., September 2000
    Waste Water Technology Fact Sheet, Low-Flow Toilets
    EPA 832-F-00-047
    Accessed 21 October 2023
    <https://www3.epa.gov/npdes/pubs/hi-eff_toilet.pdf>

Note: Newer models of toilet work very effectively using much less water, though some early low-flow toilet models were not very effective in flushing properly.

11. Architectural Digest, 6 February 2024
    architecturaldigest.com, What's the Average Solar Panel Payback Period?
    Accessed 16 March 2024
    <https://www.architecturaldigest.com/reviews/solar/solar-panel-payback-period>

12. Direct Energy
    How Much Electricity Does My Refrigerator Use?
    Accessed 21 October 2023
    <https://www.directenergy.com/learning-center/how-much-electricity-does-my-refrigerator-use#:~:text=55%20per%20day%2C%20%2416.67%20per,only%20use%20350%20kWh%20annually.>

    Arcadia Blog, 20 July 2017
    How Much Electricity Your Refrigerator Uses
    Accessed 21 October 2023
    <https://blog.arcadia.com/much-electricity-refrigerator-uses/#:~:text=Ft%20fridge%20from%20the%20early,the%20average%20was%20533%20kWh.>

    Ontario Energy Board
    Electricity Rates
    Accessed 21 October 2023
    <https://www.oeb.ca/consumer-information-and-protec-tion/electricity-rates>

13. Energy Education
    Appliance
    Accessed 21 October 2023
    <https://energyeducation.ca/encyclopedia/Appliance>

14. Long Term Trends
    Home Price To Income Ratio (US & UK)
    Accessed 21 October 2023
    <https://www.longtermtrends.net/home-price-median-annual-income-ratio/>

15. Erica Alini, 10 April 2021
    Global News, Here Is How Home Prices Compare To Incomes Across Canada
    Accessed 21 October 2023
    <https://globalnews.ca/news/7740756/home-prices-compared-to-income-across-canada/>

16. Deborah Kearns, 19 May 2023
    Investopedia, How Much Money do I Need to Put Down on a Mortgage?
    Accessed 16 March 2024
    <https://www.investopedia.com/mortgage/mortgage-guide/down-payment/>

17. Amy Fontinelle, 24 October 2023
    Forbes, Median Home Price by State 2024
    Accessed 16 March 2024
    <https://www.forbes.com/advisor/mortgages/real-estate/median-home-prices-by-state/>

18. David Bach, *The Automatic Millionaire, Canadian Edition: A Powerful One-Step Plan to Live and Finish Rich* (Doubleday Canada, 2003).

19. Tanaya Macheel, 30 April 2022
    CNBC, Warren Buffett Gives His Most Expansive Explanation For Why He Doesn't Believe In Bitcoin
    Accessed 21 October 2023

<https://www.cnbc.com/2022/04/30/warren-buffett-gives-his-most-expansive-explanation-for-why-he-doesnt-believe-in-bitcoin.html#:~:text=He%20said%20at%20the%20Berkshire,%2C%20I%20don't%20know>

Basic Budget

Expense	Monthly Cost
Mortgage/Rent	
Groceries	
Car Gas	
Property Tax	
Utilities	
Home Maintenance	
Home Insurance	
Car Insurance	
Car Maintenance/Depreciation	
Tithe	
Clothes	
Phone	
Internet	
Professional Fees	
Gifts	
Other	
Savings	
Monthly Total	
Annual Total	

Economy of Grocery Items
(cut out for your fridge)

Cheap Healthy Foods	eggs
potatoes/sweet potatoes	chicken (whole, legs, drumsticks)
peas	cottage cheese
dried pasta	yogurt
broccoli	peanut butter
carrots (whole)	**Expensive Foods**
canned tomatoes	fresh meats (especially red meats)
frozen mixed vegetables (bulk pack)	cheeses
rice	snack foods
oatmeal	prepared foods (i.e., potato salad)
bread	frozen breaded chicken or fish
beans (dried or canned)	fruit (out of season)
bananas	cut fresh fruit
frozen berries (bulk pack)	alcoholic beverages

About the Author

John Carter founded and managed a successful student housing business between 2007-2016. He holds a BSc (Hon) from the University of Toronto, having specialized in biochemistry and minored in mathematics. He has always been interested in managing personal finances successfully and feels fortunate that his family has done well by the application of useful financial principles. He lives in beautiful Peterborough, Ontario with his wife Sheila and eight-year-old son James.

Please leave a review at amazon.com

Go to:
"Good With Money a Brief Christian Guide to Financial Stewardship". Select "write a customer review"
in the Customer Reviews section.

I hope that you have enjoyed the book, and that it will prove to serve you and those you care about well.

Made in United States
Troutdale, OR
06/04/2024

20318693R00076